RANTS FROM THE HILL

ALSO BY MICHAEL P. BRANCH

Raising Wild: Dispatches from a Home in the Wilderness

RANTS FROM THE HILL

ON PACKRATS, BOBCATS, WILDFIRES, CURMUDGEONS, A DRUNKEN MARY KAY LADY & OTHER ENCOUNTERS WITH THE WILD IN THE HIGH DESERT

MICHAEL P. BRANCH

ROOST BOOKS

BOULDER // 2017

Roost Books
An imprint of Shambhala Publications, Inc.
4720 Walnut Street
Boulder, Colorado 80301
roostbooks.com

9 8 7 6 5 4 3 2 1

First Edition
Printed in the United States of America

⊗This edition is printed on acid-free paper that meets
the American National Standards Institute Z39.48 Standard.
♻ This book is printed on 30% postconsumer recycled paper.
For more information please visit www.shambhala.com.

Distributed in the United States by Penguin Random House LLC
and in Canada by Random House of Canada Ltd

Designed by Daniel Urban-Brown

LIBRARY OF CONGRESS CATALOGING-IN-PUBLICATION DATA
Names: Branch, Michael P., author. | Branch, Michael P. Raising wild.
Title: Rants from the hill: on packrats, bobcats, wildfires, curmudgeons, a drunken Mary
Kay lady, and other encounters with the wild in the high desert / Michael P. Branch.
Description: First edition. | Boulder: Roost Books, 2017.
Identifiers: LCCN 2016053828 | ISBN 9781611804577 (paperback: acid-free paper)
Subjects: LCSH: Branch, Michael P.—Homes and haunts—Great Basin. | Wilderness
areas—Great Basin. | Deserts—Great Basin. | Branch, Michael P.—Family. | Parenting—
Great Basin. | Natural history—Great Basin. | Great Basin—Social life and customs. |
Nevada—Social life and customs. | Great Basin—Description and travel. |
Nevada—Description and travel. | BISAC: HUMOR / Form / Essays. | NATURE /
Essays. | BIOGRAPHY & AUTOBIOGRAPHY / Personal Memoirs.
Classification: LCC F789 .B74 2017 | DDC 979—dc23 LC record available at
https://lccn.loc.gov/2016053828

For my parents, Stu and Sharon Branch
without you no hill

Benedictio: May your trails be crooked, winding, lonesome, dangerous, leading to the most amazing view. May your mountains rise into and above the clouds. May your rivers flow without end, meandering through pastoral valleys tinkling with bells, past temples and castles and poets' towers into a dark primeval forest where tigers belch and monkeys howl, through miasmal and mysterious swamps and down into a desert of red rock, blue mesas, domes and pinnacles and grottos of endless stone, and down again into a deep vast ancient unknown chasm where bars of sunlight blaze on profiled cliffs, where deer walk across the white sand beaches, where storms come and go as lightning clangs upon the high crags, where something strange and more beautiful and more full of wonder than your deepest dreams waits for you—beyond that next turning of the canyon walls.

—EDWARD ABBEY, preface to the 1988
    reprint of *Desert Solitaire* (1968)

CONTENTS

THE VIEW FROM RANTING HILL

I WAS NOT ALWAYS DEVOTED to the pastoral fantasy of living in the remote high desert of the American West. Earlier in life, I worked my way through the serial pastoral fantasies of withdrawing from the din and superficiality of overcivilization to a rustic life in the Blue Ridge Mountains, by the Atlantic seashore, and in a Florida swamp. But I like to think that I have become more focused over time, as I succumbed and committed to the driest and most impossible of pastoral fantasies more than twenty years ago: I am now a confirmed desert rat.

It might be said that all things pastoral are a form of fantasy, in the sense that our escapist dreams are our least achievable and most necessary. But there was something especially irrational about my passionate desire to retreat to a landscape as extreme and inhospitable as the one that became my home. The Great Basin is the largest of American deserts, a 190,000-square-mile immensity of alien territory that rolls out from the Rockies west to the Sierra Nevada, bordered on the north by the Columbia Plateau and down south by those better-known deserts, the Mojave and Sonoran. From this inconceivably vast desert basin no drop of water ever reaches the sea. Out here in northern Nevada, on the far western edge of the Great Basin, we live in the rain shadow of the Sierra, which limits our annual precipitation to about seven inches. Because the elevation is almost 6,000 feet it is cold here as well as hot, subject to blizzard as well as wildfire, and characterized by extremes of weather and temperature unmatched by any other US state.

While environmental writers often deploy the metaphor of falling in love to evoke a magical moment of intimacy with a natural landscape, the Great Basin Desert is so titanic, inhospitable, and unwelcoming that the urge to dwell here is not easily understood, even by those of us who have chosen to act on it. Given that pastoral fantasies remain perpetually vulnerable to threats as simple as bad weather or the need for a day job, my attempt at bucolic retreat in this land of wildfire, hypothermia, desiccation, and rattlers might seem ill-advised. But the sheer vastness and starkness of this place attracted me and then worked on me slowly, over time, like wind on rock, until I had no ambition greater than to make a life in these high, dry wilds.

Finding the way out here was a long, challenging process. Initially, my wife, Eryn, and I moved to a semirural area about fifteen miles northwest of Reno, Nevada. There we hiked, gardened, and played music but also worked, saved, and planned, always eyeing a move even farther into the hinterlands. After several years, we had saved enough to begin our search for a piece of raw land in a spectacular but isolated area of desert hills and canyons adjacent to public lands and at the foot of a stunning, split-summited, 8,000-foot mountain. Because it was so distant, high-elevation, fire-prone, and so frequently rendered inaccessible by snow, mud, and terrible roads, land in this area was relatively inexpensive—and because water is the name of the game here and only one well is permitted per parcel, large pieces of land were only marginally more expensive than smaller ones.

After a search that lasted several years, we purchased a hilly, 49.1-acre parcel near the end of an awful, 2.3-mile-long, nearly impassable dirt road. The land had no well, no building pad, and no access road, but it was wild, alluring, and very close to Bureau of Land Management (BLM) lands stretching all the way to the foot of the Sierra Nevada in neighboring California. For several more years, as we saved up to build, we visited the property regularly—hiking, working to reduce fuels to prepare for wildfire, and considering where a house might someday be constructed. Before long, we cut a narrow, sinuous driveway, a half-mile-long strip of perilous caliche mud that wound to the top of a prominent hill at the back of the parcel. There, we later sunk a well and cleared a small patch of sagebrush and burned-over juniper snags in hopes of someday making a home. To help us visualize the house, I drove rebar stakes along the perimeter of the would-be structure and connected them with twine. We often trekked up to the site, opened camp chairs somewhere within the twine house, and imagined what it would be like to someday sit in that spot within our home, taking in that particular view of the distant, snowcapped mountains.

In partnership with my family, and with my dad serving as our chief designer and general contractor, we eventually succeeded in designing and building a passive-solar home on the high hill at the back of our land. But life has a way of starting the next thing before you can quite finish the one you were working on. By the time we moved into our new home on New Year's Day 2004, we had become parents—a life change that puts pastoral fantasies in an entirely different light. Somehow our wild, romantic, and profoundly uninformed decision to embrace such an extreme mode of living now seemed even more extreme with ten-month-old Hannah Virginia in tow, and even the twenty-five-mile drive to town to buy diapers and whiskey (the first of which necessitates the second) seemed daunting. The realization that we might be in over our heads dawned with our second morning on the hill, when I began a mental list of all the local critters either large enough to eat or poisonous enough to kill our baby girl. Mountain lions, bobcats, and coyotes. Rattlers for sure. Possibly scorpions. Maybe a stray black bear from the nearby Sierra. Out here, great horned owls eviscerate six-pound, black-tailed jackrabbits, and golden eagles with seven-and-a-half-foot wingspans prey on pronghorn antelope fawns, so I was not entirely sure our kid would be safe even from the birds. But Hannah pulled through just fine and was joined, nearly four years later, by little sister Caroline Emerson. The four of us have been living a very challenging, gratifying, and uncommon life up here ever since.

In a media landscape that appears increasingly fragmented, ideological, and scientifically uninformed, *High Country News* has produced reliable, detailed, thoughtful, and well-written long-form environmental journalism about the American West since 1970. I had long been a subscriber when, in the spring of 2010, the folks at the magazine invited me to contribute a monthly column to their online edition. They offered me a great deal of creative freedom, and it was from that room to roam that the essays in the "Rants from the Hill" series emerged. The concept was simple: I would send missives about land and life from our remote hill in the western Great Basin Desert, and I would do so in a voice and with an angle of vision that would add a new perspective to the magazine's longstanding engagement of natural environments in the West.

Since that time I have written a big stack of small essays about our unusual life here on Ranting Hill, and out in the nearby canyons, playas, and mountains. The book you now hold is an embodiment of the "Rants from the Hill" series, although the essays have been selected, revised, resequenced, and, in many cases, renamed. This book is now a collection of what Walt Whitman called "specimen days": the essays are representative moments of encounter with the places, weather, characters, flora, and fauna of our remote corner of northwestern Nevada's high desert.

In his 1841 essay "Self-Reliance," Ralph Waldo Emerson wrote, "I would write on the lintels of the door-post, *Whim.*" I have been guided by that spirit of spontaneity in composing the Rants, which have emerged organically from the events, ideas, characters (both human and nonhuman), and experiences that have, over time, come to make up my shared life with Eryn and our daughters on Ranting Hill. In this sense, the fires and floods, mountain lions and bobcats, rattlers and scorpions—even the eccentric rural neighbors—wrote themselves into the Rants simply by making appearances in our life. Although the events and characters I describe have been sculpted with the tools of creative nonfiction and often spun into shape on the lathe of humor, they are grounded in our very real experiences here in the remote foothills of the western Great Basin.

Three driving concerns inspire this book. The first has to do with the longstanding, centuries-old misperception of deserts in the American cultural imaginary. It has rarely been necessary to explain to Americans why a mountain, river, lake, forest, meadow, or seashore is a beautiful place. We have long seen such places celebrated on Sierra Club calendars and in bad oil paintings on motel walls. Arid lands have not fared as well in the American environmental imagination, and even among deserts—which are arguably the most maligned natural landscapes in North America—the Great Basin has been doubly disenfranchised. This vast country lacks the postcard red-rock arches of southern Utah, the epic majesty of Arizona's Grand Canyon, or even the saguaro-sentineled sandscapes so often represented in American cinema—a fact attributable less to the undeniable beauty of the Mojave than to its economically convenient proximity to the dream factory of Hollywood.

The Great Basin is immense and sublimely beautiful, but as with all things sublime, it can inspire feelings of unfamiliarity, vulnerability, and even fear—feelings that engender an environmental aesthetic that has caused this high desert to be too often viewed as a barren wasteland, rather than as the rich and biodiverse network of natural interrelationships that it actually is. Unfortunately, that landscape aesthetic has very real environmental consequences. For example, it is no accident that during the Cold War Nevada was chosen as the place to detonate nine hundred nuclear weapons, or that Yucca Mountain has, for decades now, been the proposed repository of the nation's high-level radioactive waste. While I do not intend the Rants to solve such political problems, I do hope they highlight the unfortunate and sometimes dangerous connections between our misperceptions of desert lands and how we ultimately choose to understand and treat those lands.

My second abiding concern is how often environmental narratives willfully erase families and children from the scene. Beginning with the earliest literary adventures—from James Fenimore Cooper's *The Pioneers* (1823) and Herman Melville's *Moby-Dick* (1851) to Theodore Roosevelt's *Ranch Life and the Hunting-trail* (1888) and John Muir's *My First Summer in the Sierra* (1911)—wild places have often been represented as the province of men, while masculinity has been characterized as a form of brave solitude that could only be tested fully against the life-threatening power of nature. Both the fictional and real heroes of American environmental literature have often been men in flight not only from the pressures of civilized life but also from their roles as husbands, fathers, and neighbors. But I am no Natty Bumppo, Rip Van Winkle, Ishmael, or Huck Finn—no Henry David Thoreau, Edward Abbey, Everett Ruess, or Christopher Mc-Candless. Although I value solitude and walk well over 1,000 wilderness miles each year without company, my primary connection to nature is through my family and, especially, through shared experiences with our daughters. To the degree that the canon of environmental writing has depended upon narratives of solitude to valorize intimacy with the natural world, it has failed to account for what is most important in many of our lives: family. My favorite endorsement of the Rants essays came from an editor at *High Country News* who claimed, "If Thoreau drank more whiskey and lived in the desert, he'd write like this." Much as I embrace and treasure this characterization, for it to be accurate it must expand to imagine an arid-lands literary descendant of Thoreau who, like John Muir, loves the wild but is also a husband and the father of two daughters.

Finally, I hope the Rants demonstrate the pleasure, power, and poignancy of humor as a redemptive mode of engagement with the natural world. Environmental discourse has long been dominated by the jeremiad and the elegy—stylized, often predictable forms of expression that emphasize either our anger in the face of environmental degradation or our mourning in response to both immediate and impending environmental loss. With respect to the ongoing environmental crisis, let me be the first to say that anyone who is not angry and sad about current affairs is simply not paying attention. But there are substantial liabilities to environmental writing that is relentless in its insistence that we attend only to what is wounded and not also benefit from the regenerative potential of meaningful contact with place. Our default may be to feel that humor is an ineffective or perhaps even an inappropriate response to the degraded environmental conditions in which we find ourselves—that to welcome laughter is the moral equivalent of fiddling while Rome burns. I disagree. Humor not only is an effective means of examining our own behavior and exposing flaws in our culture's most misguided values and destructive practices, but also functions as a crucial mode of self-reflection and self-protection. The comic is a life-giving force, because comedy encourages resilience and thus helps us to combat despair. As a writer, I believe that the craft of humor is an essential element of the art of survival.

In addition to these primary drivers—appreciation for deserts, inclusion of families, and an embrace of humor—the Rants reveal a wide range of other preoccupations. Among these I count the power of place to shape one's character and sensibility; the relationship between human and nonhuman animals; the correlation between material nature and the language used to describe it; the difficulty of balancing a desire for freedom and solitude with a need for social interdependence; the fascinating, idiosyncratic characters who are both attracted to and produced by isolated modes of dwelling; the power of imagining the land up and down a range of geological and temporal scales; the environmental consequences of culturally devaluing certain landscape types; the tension between childhood and adult perceptions of the natural world; and, the myriad ways in which, try as we might, our assumptions about nature are usually wrong.

At the heart of this book, though, is my fascination with the durability of pastoral fantasy. I confess that living in the remote high desert has been rather hard on my own idyllic dream of retreat. But, as dwelling here has stripped me of illusions I held about both nature and myself, it has given in exchange a new, highly textured sense of the world that is more real and equally fantastic.

As you turn to these Rants, kindly remember that only recently has the wonderful word *rant* come to mean "a long, angry, or impassioned speech; a tirade." Instead, I invoke *rant* in its earlier, nobler form. Starting around 1600, to *rant* meant to express oneself in "an extravagant or hyperbolical manner"—with the important caveat that this was understood to be a *good* thing. The archaic noun form is even more cheering, as a *rant* was "a boisterous, lively, or riotous scene or occasion; a festive gathering; a romp, a spree." It is in that spirit that I share the thirty-seven literary missives that comprise *Rants from the Hill.*

THE GHOST OF SILVER HILLS

YOU MAY RECALL the novelist William Faulkner's famous Yoknapatawpha County, which, though fictional, was based upon the Mississippi town in which Faulkner lived. Well, I'm ready to give a fictional name to my own real home place: Silver Hills, Nevada. Silver Hills is much like Yoknapatawpha, only with a little less incest and a lot less rain.

I live with my wife and our two daughters in the western Great Basin Desert, at 6,000 feet, on the eastern slope of the Sierra Nevada Mountains, on a desiccated hilltop so mercilessly exposed to wind, snow, and fire that our house appears to lean away from the trouble, like a juniper canted by the constant blast of the Washoe Zephyr. It is a stark and extreme landscape, one that shows no concern for our flourishing or even our survival. To us, it is the most remarkable home imaginable.

A decade ago, when we first scouted the rural high desert where we ultimately bought land and later built our home, there weren't many folks out here from whom to get stories of whatever and whomever might have come before. We knew from the obsidian arrowheads we occasionally found on prominent outcroppings that, in the deep past, this was Northern Paiute hunting grounds, and the quartz-rimmed test holes dotting the steepest foothills marked the moment when silver prospectors had come and gone. But the recent human history of Silver Hills—from the era before the main road was paved and power brought in—consisted of little more than rusty, old, church key–style beer cans found beneath the sage. Among the few neighbors who had moved out here ahead of the grid, only scraps of stories remained. There was the day a black bear cub strayed over from the Sierra and terrified somebody's dogs, and the night a huge wildfire crested a nearby ridge and broke like a scarlet tsunami, flooding the valley with flames. Some folks said that a small plane had once crashed in the hills nearby—and that the pilot had survived and simply walked out of this rugged country—though nobody recalled the details. One old off-the-gridder told me that twenty years ago a neighbor who built on a remote BLM inholding had kept an elephant as a pet, though with this tale, as with all others, there never seemed to be anything behind the stories but more stories.

An unconfirmed legend that touched my family more directly was that of a man who was rumored to have lived on the land—just camping out in the desert someplace, it was said—in an area near the parcel we ultimately bought. But the follow-up questions I asked of the old-timers led nowhere. No one knew who the man was or why he had been out here or where exactly he had camped. One neighbor claimed that the man's campfire had eventually drawn attention from the sheriff, who traced the smoke plume to the man's camp and moved him off the land. Another neighbor swore, instead, that the man had simply vanished, like a ghost.

A few years after purchasing our land, we designed and built a passive-solar, wood-heated home, which we occupied about the time of our first daughter's first birthday. I didn't think any more about the mysterious camper than I did about the crashed plane or the pet elephant, and I discovered no evidence to corroborate any of these local legends. In those first two years, I tramped several thousand miles in the nearby hills and canyons, until I felt I had found every juniper stump and packrat midden, every erratic boulder and red tail hunting perch within ten miles of home. I knew where the pronghorn moved and where the ravens nested, which arroyos were too snaky in summer and which were wind-protected in winter.

Then, during the early spring of our third year out here, I was walking on our property when I decided to take shelter from a biting wind that was driving a late-season snow. I clambered down a rocky slope about a quarter mile from the house and got down on all fours to crawl into a copse of junipers that was too dense to be entered upright. After creeping eight or ten feet through the dirt, I discovered an opening in the center of the stand—a small, clear area that was ringed by an impenetrable halo of tangled trees. Suddenly, I realized what I had stumbled upon. In the center of the small clearing was a perfect circle of blackened rocks that had once been a fire pit, and next to it was a tidy pile of short juniper logs that looked as if they had been stacked that morning. Dangling from the higher boughs were strands of old cordage, which had at one time tethered a canvas tarp that was now half buried in the duff along with what appeared to be a timeworn bedroll. Beneath one of the trees was a small mountain of beer bottles, which I recognized from my youth as having contained Miller High Life—clear bottles from the dark days so long before the microbrew revolution that Miller could be called "the champagne of beers."

The most surprising item in this remarkable, wild digs was stacked neatly beneath one corner of the tarp: an impressive cache of surprisingly well-preserved Nixon-era *Playboy* magazines. In effect, I had made the astounding anthropological discovery of a western Great Basin Mancave, circa 1973. The cover of the September 1970 issue featured a blonde woman wearing a leather headband and wide macramé belt, accoutered with fringed purse, and flashing not her exposed breasts but rather a peace sign, which she displayed before breasts so completely obscured by a tasteful blue sweater that the entire effect resembled less *Playboy* than *Good Housekeeping*. Readers of the October 1971 issue were greeted by a cheerful woman with an enormous afro whose body was thoroughly obscured by a white plastic chair resembling the head of giant bunny. The cover of the 1972 Christmas issue didn't even deploy a photograph, instead offering a stylized drawing of a woman dressed as Santa Claus—though she did look considerably less grouchy than a Santa at the mall often does.

What would this place have been like in, say, the early spring of 1973, when the ghost of Silver Hills sat alone by a crackling juniper log fire, hoisting Millers and fantasizing about whether he would prefer to share his sylvan sanctuary with the righteous hippie chick or the smiling stone fox with the huge afro? There would have been no home within several miles and no paved road within ten, and it was then a twenty-mile walk to the edge of town. Was he on the lam? Or was he, like me, simply a man who had chosen the hills and canyons over some other life? Was his juniper-bowered Mancave an indication of his sanity, or the lack of it? Would it be accurate to call him homeless, or was this his true home? Was he trying to get to someplace else or only hoping, as I so often do, that someplace else wouldn't catch up with him out here?

The ghost of Silver Hills had chosen the perfect spot, the kind of snug shelter where one might well wait out the Nixon administration—or a parole officer or creditor, or the draft board, or the millennium, or whatever else might need waiting out. As I huddled within the ghost's magic circle, sheltered from the blowing snow, I felt a sudden urge to kindle a small blaze of aromatic juniper, crack a sparkling High Life, and do some light reading until the gloaming swallowed these windswept desert hills.

A THOUSAND-MILE
WALK TO HOME

EIGHT YEARS AGO THIS SPRING, I blew out a lumbar disc
while running a jackhammer in the desert near my house—
an accident that was the result of simple bad luck, with the odds
skewed by the fact that a jackhammer was the wrong tool for the
job and that alcohol may have been involved. After a long, miser-
able recovery period during which I was as ornery as a walleyed
mule, I finally mended enough that Eryn could get me out of the
house, which was a great relief to her.

As I began to get back on my feet, Eryn asked what turned out
to be one of the best questions I have ever received: "Bubba, now
that you're finally healing, how do you want your life to be different from before the injury?"

My reply was immediate and spontaneous. "I just want to walk
and walk and walk."

In that moment, I came up with an idea that was absurdly arbitrary: I would walk 1,000 miles in the next 365 days, and I would
start every walk from home—an approach that was practical, since

we live adjacent to BLM lands stretching all the way to California. Why 1,000 miles in a year? A better question seemed to be, *Why the hell not?* I had not one single good reason, no justification, not a hint of a plan. Nor did I have any idea how far 1,000 miles really is, though it sounded like a lot. But once I started to break it down, I realized that I would not need to pull heroic, big-mile days of the sort long-trail hikers on the nearby Pacific Crest Trail do. While 1,000 miles sounds impressive, it amounts to just 2.74 miles per day, which seems incredibly modest. Just 2.74? I reckoned plenty of people probably walk their poodles farther than that in their suburban neighborhoods.

Within two weeks of walking toward my goal, however, I realized that 2.74 was the wrong number to have focused on. The number that mattered, as it turned out, was 365. It is rugged country out here, and if you subtract from 365 the number of days we have scorching heat, deep snow, blasting winds, or raging wildfire, you are down to approximately the number 7, and I had to admit that seven 143-mile walks seemed daunting. If I was going to get to 1,000 miles, it was not going to be as a weekend warrior—I had to approach these short desert hikes as something that happened every day no matter what. And so I was forced to rethink my experiment, which now seemed less about walking than about practice, in the same sense that a monk must meditate in the temple each morning or a bassist must rehearse every afternoon.

And that is how walking became for me a discipline that I practiced each day, regardless of mood or conditions. When the snow grew too deep to posthole the 2.74, I snowshoed it. If the blasting wind shotgunned sand up from the desert floor, I wore ski goggles. When temperatures soared to triple digits, I hiked by moonlight. Once, when an earthquake hit while I was walking, I was forced to squat down until the tremors subsided; then I stood back up and just kept walking.

I also walked in ways that would earn the censure of most nature writers, who insist earnestly that each saunter should be an ennobling, Thoreauvian pilgrimage that hones our attention to the natural world. I did take hundreds of walks of this ennobling variety, but many were far less solemn. If the San Francisco Giants were playing, I listened not to the breeze as it finned dried balsamroot leaves, but rather to the crack of the bat as it channeled in through my earbuds. One day while doing fuels reduction for fire control, I weed-whacked more than half of the 2.74—not very Thoreauvian, I'm afraid. That first year, I walked at least 100 miles pushing baby Caroline in her off-road stroller (which I customized by equipping it with knobby tires, slimed to protect against puncture by desert peach thorns), and I may have skipped at least four miles of that first thousand with our older daughter, Hannah. On days when I had been made to suffer fools in town, I ritually drank 2.74 beers as I walked.

It wasn't long before I not only managed to fit in these daily walks but could not survive without them. For the past eight years, I have continued the thousand-mile annual walks, which are exactly as arbitrary and as gratifying as they were when I began. Because I actually averaged more like 1,300 miles per year, the miles I walked in those years could have taken me all the way from the Great Basin down to Key West, where I might have enjoyed a bowl of conch chowder and a good spiced rum before rambling up to the coast of Maine to eat fresh lobster and drink imperial IPA. Then I could have hiked from there over to Montana to do a little fly-fishing, after which I'd still have enough miles leftover to saunter back down to New Orleans and catch a late set at the Bourbon Street Blues Club before walking across Texas and the American Southwest and back to my home in the western Great Basin.

But my miles did not tend that way. They were all walked here, in the high desert, on public lands, within a ten-mile radius of Ranting Hill. If my bioregionalist experiment of walking more than 1,000 local miles each year has involved weed-whackers and beer and skipping as well as pronghorn and golden eagles and the wordless beauty of moonlight gleaming on unbroken snowfields, that may be just as well. It is incremental work, but I have had a glimpse of how these walks might someday add up to a journey, in the same way that a life is composed only of individual days, which are themselves nothing more than a series of moments in which we choose to take a small step, or do not.

CUSTOMER CRANKY

ONE OF THE FEW THINGS that connects those of us out here in the remote desert West with the rest of the world is the US Postal Service, though here in Silver Hills the experience of the mail smacks more of Dante than it does Norman Rockwell. First of all, our mailbox is almost three miles from the house, and the road between is a tortuous gumbo of mud in winter and a jaw-rattling washboard in summer. Since the four seasons here are distinguished by mud, fire, dust, and snow, we can usually walk to the mailbox about as fast as we can drive to it. The mailbox itself is so constantly blasted by wind, snow, and buckshot that it is good for little besides keeping black widows out of the weather. Then there is the troubling matter of our postal delivery person, whom Ludde, my closest neighbor and a wonderful old curmudgeon, unceremoniously calls "Femailman"—a title I would reject as rude if it weren't better than "the carrier," which, given this lady's virulent personality, is less respectful but also more accurate.

The week we moved out to Silver Hills I spotted an ancient, mud-brown Jeep creeping along the crooked row of mailboxes out at the paved road. It had no lights, signs, or insignia to indicate affiliation with the US government—probably a wise safety measure here in the land of libertarians, cranksters, survivalists, and UFO conspiracy theorists—but the arm swinging out the open window and plunging into the boxes made plain that this was, in fact, the mail. In that moment two things struck me as odd. First, the hairy arm delivering the mail ended in a hand with long, red fingernails. Second, the back window of the Jeep was lined with stuffed animals, which might have been cute back in town but was disturbingly out of place here. As the furry arm filled the last mailbox and the jeep sped away, a guy driving by in a pickup slowed down just enough to shout at me through his open window, "Don't let those teddy bears fool you!"

I learned a lot about our new neighbors during those first few months in Silver Hills, because Femailman delivered us everybody's mail but our own. Among the magazines popular out here are *Guns and Ammo* and *MuleyCrazy* (for deer hunters), although one guy also received the dubiously named *Garden and Gun* magazine. Several people subscribed to the Libertarians' even more dubiously named magazine, *Reason*, and *Off Road* was common. My favorite was the neighbor whose address received both *Antique Doll Collector* and *Hustler*, and, for some reason, I always enjoyed it when those two arrived on the same day.

Each day Eryn or I returned to our mailbox, raised the rusty red flag, and replaced the misdelivered mail, along with a polite note explaining the problem for the benefit of Femailman. But, after six months, she was still batting under .300. Eventually, we called the local post office, explained the issue, and were assured that a supervisor would talk with the carrier, who would then affix a special label to the inside of our mailbox as a reminder to them of the pattern of delivery problems. The next morning, our home phone rang at 4:45 A.M., which is so painfully close to o'dark thirty that it took me a moment to realize that it was Femailman on the line. She had just called to apologize, she said, but she sounded suspiciously unremorseful. When I pointed out that it was not yet daybreak, she abruptly hung up. That afternoon, we opened our mailbox to find the official US Postal Service decal inside, just as promised. On it, in the space left open for the postal employee to record the "PROBLEM," Femailman had noted, simply, "CUSTOMER CRANKY."

After that, however, our mail service did improve substantially, and I found, to my surprise, that I missed the guilty pleasure of perusing *Antique Doll Collector* or the magazine for retired prison guards—and I wondered if somewhere in the nearby hills someone was disappointed to no longer be receiving my Baileys chainsaw catalogue, *Beer Advocate* magazine, and *High Country News*. I even came to appreciate the label inside our mailbox, and, at least two evenings a week, I would come home from a lousy day at work to check the mail, notice the tag, and agree that Femailman was right about me after all.

That was years ago, and while I do still get *MuleyCrazy* now and then, Femailman more or less gets the right stuff in our box. Recently, though, we have had a new and very specific problem: We're receiving all our mail except for Eryn's *New Yorker*, which the publisher swears they send dutifully to our correct address each week and which they report has never been returned. When I called the local post office to explain the problem, the supervisor I spoke with hesitated, and then asked politely, "Does it say 'New York' right on the cover?"

"Well, yeah," I answered, wondering where she was headed.

"OK, I'll do what I can," she said, "but you got to understand some of these carriers don't much like that stuff from back East."

I thought for a long moment about how best to reply. Then, like the true Silver Hillbilly I have become, I said, "Yeah, that makes sense." After all, I didn't want to be cranky. Femailman still won't deliver the magazine, but I keep up the subscription, because I like to imagine that somewhere out in these sere, brown hills, a red-nailed, hairy arm is lining the cat pan with a fresh cover of *The New Yorker* every Friday afternoon.

TRAPPING THE BEES

A FEW YEARS AGO, at just this lovely, springtime season of the year, I had to go back East for a few months of work. When I returned home to Ranting Hill, which I missed mightily while I was away, I noticed plenty of changes. Great horned owls had taken up hunting perches on the peaks of our roof and had knocked back the local population of packrats. My native shrubs had survived, though they had been cropped by black-tailed jackrabbits. It was clear from scat and hoof prints that both mule deer and pronghorn antelope had grazed our property regularly. But the most obvious difference was that a thousand honeybees were buzzing around the eaves at the southwestern corner of the house.

Honeybees are unusual here in the high desert. Although we do have some forage plants—including snowberry, rabbitbrush, balsamroot, and a few wild mustards—we simply do not have enough year-round forage to make this severe desert environment very appealing to your average honeybee. I had not seen a thousand bees total in a decade up here on Ranting Hill, so it was clear that something was out of the ordinary.

Upon closer inspection, the bees were going in and out of a small hole in the eaves, where they adjoined the exterior stucco wall. When I called the local extension agent, she immediately asked, "Did you spray them yet?" When I replied that I had not, she sounded relieved. She then asked, "Are they still swarming? I mean, are they in a big clump? A swarm can be nabbed and moved pretty easily." I explained that the bees were, instead, flying in and out of the house. "Well, you're talking structural removal, then. Hopefully you can do a cut out, but you might have to do a trap out. Pest-control guys are clueless on this stuff, and most beekeepers don't want the hassle unless they can get an easy score on a swarm. Big Dan's your man on this."

Next, I called Big Dan—apparently a legend among local bee freaks—who also asked, "Spray yet?" and "Still swarming?" before patiently posing a number of other astute questions and, finally, agreeing to come out that afternoon to see if he could help. Let me admit straightaway that, as a desert rat, I know diddly squat about bees or beekeeping. I pictured Big Dan as a dude who would step down from a shiny, white F-350 looking like an astronaut in his fancy bee-fighting gear. Instead, a tiny, ancient, sunfaded, powder-blue hatchback Honda Civic rolled up, and out of it rose a man who was not only tall and large, but also graced with an immense, bushy red beard and a long braid of red hair trailing down between his shoulder blades. He was costumed not in studly bee-wrangling gear but in Birkenstocks, baggy brown cargo shorts, and a T-shirt brightly tie-dyed with a swirl pattern. He wore small, black-rimmed glasses that were so nerdy as to be completely incongruous with his hippiefied appearance. Big Dan looked like a red-haired version of the Grateful Dead guitarist Jerry Garcia, but only if Garcia had also been your kindergarten teacher. When little Caroline asked innocently if she could call him "Dan, Dan, the Big Bee Man," Dan responded gently and sincerely, "I'd be honored." My own thought in that moment was that this guy was a high-desert original—just the kind of character I had missed so much during the time I had been away from Silver Hills.

Big Dan was a soft-spoken man, a mild giant who clearly had a deep feeling for the miracle that is the honeybee. He had the sensibility of a teacher, and he taught me a hundred things about bees while going calmly about his work. Wearing no bee-battling gear whatsoever, Dan first climbed my ladder right up into the cloud of bees, where he used a stethoscope to listen to various spots on the eaves and walls of the house. From this he diagnosed that the bees were not hived up in the eaves, where he could have done a "cut out" by sawing open the soffit and physically removing the nest. Instead, they were somewhere deep inside the interior walls of the house and thus would require a full-blown "trap out." When I asked for an explanation, Big Dan agreed to trade one for a good beer.

So first we drank and talked beer, and it turned out that Dan was not only a skilled microbrewer but also a beer competition judge of repute. Then, he turned to describing a trap out.

"A trap out takes eight weeks, sometimes more," he began. I think he noticed my grimace. "Or, you can poison the bees, risk spreading disease to other hives, and leave fifty thousand dead bees in your wall. The rotting smell won't last more than a month, but the comb and honey left behind will attract ants, wax moths, and mice. When July rolls around, you may notice honey seeping through your walls."

I handed Dan a second porter and asked him to continue. "In a trap out, we first seal all the entrances to the hive except one. Then, we cover that one door with a long, funnel-shaped screen, with the tapered end pointing away from the house. Bees will come out of the cone to go forage, but when they come home, they won't be able to find their way back into the tube. Near the small end of the cone we put a nuc box, which is a secondary hive with about five frames of brood comb, cells with eggs and larvae, and, of course, a queen and a bunch of bees. When the foragers can't find their way back into the hive inside your house, they'll give up and join the secondary colony in the nuc box. It takes a long time, because you have to wait for the colony's full cycle. First, the foragers and drones will end up in the nuc box, but then the brood that's already in your wall has to hatch and develop to the foraging stage before they'll be ready to fly out and end up joining the secondary colony. You have to be patient."

"Yeah, but what about all that pest-attracting honey that'll still be inside the house?" I asked.

"Here is the true beauty of the trap out," Dan continued, with genuine enthusiasm. "Once the colony inside your wall has failed, the bees adopted into the secondary colony will have no loyalty to it. At that point we remove the one-way cone and let the bees go back inside your house!"

I told him I would need another beer to grasp why I'd want to allow what would now be sixty or even eighty thousand bees free access to the interior walls of our home. But Dan was evangelical about the elegance of the trap out. "Bees in the nuc box will fly into your walls and rob out every last bit of wax and honey, transferring it to the new colony. They're thorough! Because there's no telling where inside your house the hive is, this is the only way to leave your place clean. So, what'll it be?"

"Trap out, for sure," I answered. "When can we start?"

Without saying a word, Dan set his porter down on our stone wall, cracked a gentle grin, and walked over to his little Honda. He opened the hatchback and lifted out a bright-white hive box, carried it back with his pointer and middle fingers curled through the eye bolt in its top, and set it down next to my beer. The humming and buzzing emerging from that box was so loud that it seemed to be vibrating. Dan then strapped on a tool belt and ascended the ladder, climbing fifteen feet up into a cloud of bees. Again, he wore no veil or protective gear, and I could see bees crawling on his shoulders and head and even gathering in his bushy, red beard.

Dan stayed aloft for a half hour, caulking holes and patiently constructing and attaching the cone-shaped screen that would guide the bees out of the house and then prevent them from re-entering it. He also screwed a large hook into the wooden eaves and attached to it a heavy-duty carabiner. He then descended the ladder, lifted the white hive box, climbed back up again, and hung the hive by snapping the carabiner through the eye bolt on the box. Next, he stapled the narrow end of the cone to the face of this dangling hive, so that bees exiting our house could not miss the alternative colony. Finally, he removed the long, rectangular block that had kept the bees bottled up in the nuc box. When he came down the ladder for the last time, Dan was wearing a wide smile beneath which flowed his flame red beard, now with at least half a dozen bees crawling through it.

Eryn, the girls, and I soon came to love having the bees around, and we watched their patterns every day for weeks. We would observe the foragers emerge from the cone early in the day, return with their legs laden with pollen in the afternoon, and circle the funnel in an attempt to find a way back in. That failing, they would "beard" on the outside of the cone for an hour or two before giving up and joining the growing secondary colony in the suspended hive box. After some weeks, the traffic subsided, and we knew the brood in the wall colony was maturing and preparing to forage. Eventually, a torrent of exiting bees resumed, and for several more weeks we had the pleasure of observing their daily missions before bees once again ceased emerging from the cone.

After a week of this inactivity, Big Dan came back up to Ranting Hill. We drank some stout before Dan removed the trap cone, and he watched with satisfaction as bees from the dangling hive reentered the house in masses. I confess that I did not find this reversal of the bee stream consoling, though I tried to imagine the alternative of having honey exuding from the interior walls of our house. After a few more weeks, the bee activity again ceased, and Dan reckoned that the house hive had been robbed clean of honey and that the new colony was established. He came out to the house a third time, savored an IPA, and then ascended the ladder. Dan sealed the bees' sole entry hole to the house, blocked the entrance to the hive box, and climbed down carefully with what was now a very heavy load. Opening the hatchback of his Honda, he lifted the colony in. There were still quite a few bees clinging to Dan's box, and as he drove away, waving to the girls, I could see him smiling and appearing not to notice—or at least not to mind—the single honeybee that was still attached to his forehead.

The trap out was a wonderful reminder that often the best solution to a confrontation with nature is to work with, rather than against, the problem. Bees in our house was the problem, but it turned out that bees in our house was also the elegant solution to it. Instead of a sagging wall full of pesticide-soaked, rotting bees and rancid honeycomb, I had clean walls and a story to tell. But it was even better than that, because I learned so much about bees and was able to give Hannah and Caroline the wonderful experience of living with their own "pet" colony—even if it was suspended fifteen feet in the air. I also had the pleasure of meeting a fine high-desert character in Dan, Dan, the Big Bee Man, who later gifted us a jar of the sweet honey produced within the walls of our own home.

FERAL CHILD

AFTER ERYN'S DIFFICULT and dangerous twenty-two-hour labor, Hannah Virginia, our first daughter, made her reluctant entrance and began a still-unbroken run of being a sweet, smart, thoughtful, and interesting kid. In the early years of Hannah's life, Eryn and I were in the habit of congratulating each other on what amazing parents we were. What could be wrong with all these other people, whose kids ran around screaming and climbing things, when our daughter's sole idiosyncrasy was her preference for quiet and order? We pitied those exhausted parents, whose lives more closely resembled *Lord of the Flies* than *Lord of the Rings*, and who had consequently to face so many failed attempts to tame their ungovernable urchins. For us, parenting was a gratifying affirmation that, even in a world of chaos and noise, a rational, gentle, intelligent approach can produce a child who is delightfully well-adjusted and mercifully low-maintenance. It was this unchecked hubris that prompted us to have a second kid. After all, we were so good at parenting that doubling down seemed a sure bet.

That was before we met Caroline Emerson. Four years younger than Hannah, Caroline was born after a fast and hard labor, and has been running us ragged ever since. I suppose the middle name we chose for her may have started the trouble. Ralph Waldo Emerson is America's oldest and, to many, its most eloquent exponent of self-reliance—the belief that fierce independence, individuality, and nonconformity are the qualities we should develop in ourselves and value in others. This wild independence is precisely what we got in Caroline, though in her it is braided with an intense physicality—a remarkable strength, coordination, and spontaneous desire for adventure—that makes her appear equal parts cute little girl, Hollywood stunt double, and simian beast.

At two weeks old, Caroline launched herself out of her grandma's lap; at ten months, she stood up and walked away from us; at four years, she insisted that monkey bars should be built in place of sidewalks, because she can cover ground faster when "it's just swinging." It is a major accomplishment to persuade her to operate, even occasionally, on the horizontal surfaces of the world, and her innate ability to climb is both terrifying and inspiring. Caroline can scramble up anything: trees, fences, walls, and—in one of our best father-daughter party tricks—even *me*. I stand perfectly still as Caroline leaps onto my chest, momentarily hugging me like a sloth, after which she wedges her orangutan toes into my hipbones and then, reaching for my neck, buries her chimpanzee fingers under my collarbone and swings herself up onto my shoulders in a single, graceful motion, like an organ grinder's monkey hopping onto a pony's back. Having summited "Daddy Mountain," Caroline pumps her fists in the air and shouts, *"BOOOYAAAH!"*

Ranting Hill and its surrounding wilderness provide the ideal habitat for a little girl who is so thoroughly animal—though I often wonder whether it is Caroline's wildness that makes her the perfect inhabitant of Silver Hills or whether this remote, high-desert landscape has instead produced the wildness that is so unmistakable in her. To her, this arid wilderness is home, and town is a place you go only when you have no choice. Caroline does not mind the extreme cold out here, or the blistering heat, or the incessant wind. She hates proper clothes and coming in for supper. She loves chasing jackrabbits and searching for scorpions, and she relishes the night sounds of shrill coyote yelps and raspy owl hoots. In early spring, she wants to spot sagebrush buttercup, sand lily, and death camas—signs of the changing season here—and her main goal is to find an antler shed by a mule deer. Her favorite summer activity is scrambling up into scratchy Utah junipers, where she builds stick nests that she hopes ravens will occupy. In fall, she is the only one in our family who welcomes the return of the big wind, because she insists it is alive, and her main worry is that she may not glimpse the mountain lion that hunted our valley last autumn. In winter, she watches constantly for pronghorn, and she sleds madly down Ranting Hill, even though it is impossible to do so without crashing into thickets of ephedra and gooseberry. Her favorite winter activity is taking off her clothes, running outside, and making naked angels in the snow.

Caroline is like any normal kid, except that she wears no clothes and refuses to come indoors to pee. Though the very idea now seems hilarious, a few years ago we tried a last-ditch effort to civilize her by taking her to ballet lessons in town. When she was asked by her dance teacher to play the role of a butterfly in the class recital, she refused, explaining coolly that she would not be anything that can be eaten by a western kingbird. Instead, she set the terms for her participation: she would be happy join the recital, but only if she could be a northern harrier.

The humbling experience of living with Caroline Emerson has cured us of our delusional belief that we are, in any way, gifted as parents. An endearing term like *feisty* does not do justice to

Caroline, who is so fiercely independent, energetic, and stubborn that she is, for all practical purposes, unparentable. Her signature reply when asked to do anything she prefers not to do is to adopt the stance of a boxer—turned sideways, with one foot in front of the other, fists circling slowly—and growl, "You want some of this, huh?" The other day when she struck her pugilist pose, I said, "Give it your best shot!" She instantly launched a roundhouse left, but I deftly caught her little fist in my right palm; she followed with a savage right uppercut, which I managed to grasp in my left hand. In this moment, I believed foolishly that I had neutralized her attack. Caroline just smiled and then, before I could respond, launched herself forward and rammed the crown of her head into my groin, doubling me over and leaving me gasping for air. "*BA-BAAAM!*" she hollered, holding up her puny arms in a would-be biceps flex.

Unlike Hannah, her professorial big sister, for whom all actions are preceded by thorough analysis of contingencies and consequences, Caroline takes a "ready, fire, aim" approach to being in the world. Her instinct is always to try something to see if it will work, rather than to think—or, even worse, to *talk*—about whether it might work, and she views the basic risk analyses inherent to parenting as just so much cowardly stalling, hedging, and jawflappery. While this attitude has a substantial downside—one made clear when she once leapt into the Pacific Ocean several years in advance of learning how to swim—it is impossible not to admire her unrelenting, visceral drive to experience the world. In the time it takes me and Eryn to discuss whether it is safe to allow Caroline to climb a particular tree, she has already reached its top. While we think, she acts; while we calculate, she executes; while we wonder what she might be capable of, she sets out immediately to find out. Caroline is more her own person than any adult I know, and her spontaneous confidence provides a salutary challenge to the deadening logic of a grown-up world in which things are as they are only because that is how they have always been—because some adult who was afraid to try something in their own way could not dream up a better reply than "because I said so."

The word *wild* derives from the Old English *wilde*, which means "in the natural state, uncultivated, untamed, undomesticated, uncontrolled." But the word's older root is in the Latin *ferus*, which gives rise to the English word *fierce*, which is itself a cousin to the delightful word *feral*. It is this quality of being feral that fascinates me most, for while a wild animal has no experience of enclosure or constraint, a feral animal will "run wild, having escaped from domestication." Caroline Emerson began her escape from domestication—began going feral—the moment she was born. We can give Caroline a home, but she will be in the blast of the desert wind most of the time. We can dress her in warm clothes, but she is going to peel them off and sprint outside to leave angels in the snow. As our family's half-wild emissary to the more-than-human realm, Caroline seems to have entered this high-desert landscape through a snowstorm or a lenticular cloud or a secret green door beneath the sage. She is the girl for whom the walls the world has built around her exist merely to hold up the wild doors that only she can see.

GROUND TRUTHING THE PEACEABLE KINGDOM

L AST NIGHT, I lay awake in bed listening to the sound of little claws scrabbling inside the walls of our house. Because the sheetrock acts as a drumhead, amplifying sounds that originate within the wall, the scratching is disturbingly loud. It sounds as if there is an irate raccoon in there, which is how I know it is only a mouse; if it were a big packrat, as it sometimes is, it would sound like a terrified person trapped behind the wall, evoking the chilling entombments of an Edgar Allan Poe tale.

Tonight, the packrats are on the outside of the house, where I hear them racing along the stucco walls before pausing to clean their whiskers. In the morning, their turds will litter the stoops, and their urine will stain the windowsills, as if someone had spilled a pint of porter there. For now, I try to lull myself to sleep with the dim hope that rye whiskey might provide an effective inoculation against Hantavirus.

"Ground truthing," a term used by environmental activists, re- fers to the important process of comparing a representation of the land (for example, one that appears in writing, photographs, or maps) with actual conditions on the land, and then measuring and recording the inevitable gap between the two. When we bought this isolated piece of land and planned to build our home and life here, we understood that we were choosing to live among the wild critters. But, like most folks who pursue a pastoral fantasy, we had not ground truthed it; that is, we did not have a solid idea of what we were actually signing up for. I am unsure what I imagined back then, when my idealized vision of desert dwelling was obscured by the golden haze that surrounds all untried plans, but I suppose my rural dream was equal parts Retreat from the Vices of Over-civilization, Enter the Peaceable Kingdom, and Wear Only Boxer Shorts and a Coonskin Cap. These are dangerous fantasies when indulged individually, but in combination they have proven especially perilous.

For the past decade, every assumption I ever made about nature has been challenged, every environmental value I held tested, and every elaborate self-image I constructed slowly eroded away by living amid fire, blizzard, and wind. Out here in the desert West, the lion does not lie down with the lamb; instead, the mountain lion prowls by night and tries to eat your dog and cat. We tree huggers find very few trees to embrace around here, and those few are being used to shade Great Basin rattlers from the scorching sun. Certainly, pacifism is nowhere in sight, as the land is dotted almost as often by bones, entrails, and tufted piles of feathers as it is by desert peach, gooseberry, and rabbitbrush. Even the great horned owls, which we assumed would lull us to sleep with their gentle hooting, instead keep us wide-eyed by shrieking "whaaaa whaaaaaa-aa-aa-aarrrkk" (a direct quotation from my bird book) as they prepare to eviscerate their hapless prey.

While we humans tend to fear megafauna like bears and mountain lions, no force of nature is more daunting than rodents, which are so prolific, unrelenting, and indefatigable that, after living a few years here, I began to wish I could be fatally attacked by a mountain lion, just to have my capitulation to the rodents over with all at once. Instead, I must engage in endless and losing combat against the utterly invincible Army of Rodentia, which around here consists of platoons of field mice, kangaroo rats, bushy-tailed packrats, montane voles, antelope ground squirrels, and California ground squirrels—each of which does its special kind of damage, and none of which could be extirpated even if a Special Forces unit were suddenly dispatched by chopper to Ranting Hill.

The real problem is not the rodents but me, with my stubborn insistence upon inhabiting a place that, absent my intrusion, would have little difficulty controlling its rodent population. Even when we are gone for a few days, the owls take up hunting perches on the peaks of our roof (as evidenced by the jumbo-size, white crap blasts beneath them), the coyotes use their paws to excavate ground-squirrel tunnels, the harriers and red tails constantly threaten death from above, and even the gopher snakes move in to patrol the packrat stick nests among the junipers. It is as if all of predatory nature is simply waiting for me to get my pathetically ineffectual operation out of the way so the usual business of chomping and gulping can resume apace. By disturbing this natural cycle of predation with our presence, we have inadvertently become Ranting Hill's top predator, which means that reveries about pastoral nature must be interrupted by a lot of slaying of my fellow creatures. So much for the Peaceable Kingdom.

It is easy to prattle on about methods of "pest control," but out here there are real limits to their effectiveness. I cannot use snap traps to catch rodents, since that would risk injuring Lucy, our lazy cat, whom we adopted in the vain hope that she would do the rodent catching. I won't use poison, since this place is also home to our little girls, whom I now refer to not by name but only as "my sweet little nontarget species." Instead, I have been driven to a variety of depressingly violent strategies for protecting our home against takeover. My most innovative and elegant tactic involves a small, inground fishpond, which I installed so the girls could have a few goldfish whose bowl I would not have to clean. It turns out that rodents are wonderfully fond of suicidal drowning, which most mornings leaves the goldfish staring up at a long-tailed silhouette. Better still, a local magpie has discovered that our little pond is a rich source of carrion, and so it visits each morning to haul away the dead. Nature thus provides undertaker as well as corpse, allowing me to keep both my conscience and my hands clean.

More troubling is that my desperate determination to battle these rodents has turned me from a mild-mannered lover of nature into a gun-toting vigilante. On days when Eryn takes the girls to town and I am home alone, I undergo a disturbing transformation from a mild-mannered writer to a free-blasting hillbilly who more closely resembles Yosemite Sam than Henry Thoreau. I now use my writing desk primarily as a hunting blind, from which I rise occasionally (in my boxer shorts and coonskin cap) to fire out the window at antelope ground squirrels as they devour our plants. If you find it unconscionable that a grown man would turn a shotgun on an animal weighing five ounces, you will not be heartened to discover that another method of rodent control I employ is electrocution. In an especially desperate moment, I resorted to the online purchase of a device called a "Rat Zapper," a battery-operated death chamber that accommodates mice and smallish packrats. It is only moderately effective, but in a battle that must be waged on many fronts it has its place, not to mention that it arrived accompanied by a handsome T-shirt depicting a terrified rodent being struck in the skull by a fiery bolt of lightning. When the mice become wary of the Zapper, I resort to chasing them around the garage with the shopvac, keeping score aloud as each "tthhhwooosh-plonkk" sound registers another short journey through the esophagus of the vacuum tube. Not an easy method, but perfectible; it's all in the wrist.

My primary means of self-defense is live trapping, which I do each day and night in order to round up both the diurnal and nocturnal among my furry neighbors. To become an effective trapper, I have had to do a great deal of research into the behavioral ecology of rodents, which has immeasurably increased my appreciation for what absolute marvels of evolutionary biology these little monsters are. Their ability to adapt to extreme environments, eat almost anything, occupy diverse ecological niches, produce young at a dizzying rate that keeps them ahead of even the most voracious predators—all this and a great deal more has inspired my admiration. The irony that I have come to respect these animals even as I have learned to exterminate them is rivaled only by the more painful irony that I send them to the Elysian Fields using the unhappily named "Havahart" trap. Once rodents are live-trapped, there are few alternatives for their disposal, especially since I have resisted the temptation to release the captives a mile from here, near the home of a grouchy neighbor whom Caroline calls "Mister Grumpledumps." And so I subject the caged beasts to "swimming lessons" in my improvised hillbilly-trashcan swimming pool. Needless to say, my rodent pupils invariably fail.

If all of this sounds grisly, that's precisely the point. My home desert is not an antiseptic, pastoral retreat but rather a teeming, fecund, wild place, where we all scrabble away desperately to get the upper claw. Walden Pond is nowhere in sight, and the hard truth of life on the ground here exposes the Peaceable Kingdom for what it is: the impossible fantasy of a natural world that is not only harmonious but also bloodless.

LUCY THE DESERT CAT

AMONG MY MOST SULFUROUS and vitriolic rants are those inspired by Lucy, our family's housecat. Because we live in wild country, at high elevation, with terrible weather, surrounded by a spate of voracious predators, this is hardly a proper habitat for any cat that is not a bobcat or mountain lion. When I moved out into this vast desert to get in touch with my Inner Curmudgeon, I certainly never saw a cat in the picture. My forbearance in this case is linked to the fact that I am the father of young daughters, a condition that is 95 percent blessing and 5 percent unwanted pets. I certainly agreed to the idea of having Hannah and Caroline, but I still maintain that Eryn bringing a kitten in on their diapered coattails was taking unfair advantage of both me and my old dog, Darcy.

I hold no truck with the idea that humans can be neatly taxonomized into "dog people" and "cat people," but I suspect that my bias against cats firmed up long before Lucy the Desert Cat joined us on Ranting Hill. It has long been obvious to me that cats are unsociable misanthropes, and because I myself am reclusive and antisocial, I find these qualities intolerable in others. No reasonable person can deny that cats are sneaky and untrustworthy—even the way they slink over to their food bowl makes them look suspicious, as if they just robbed a liquor store or snatched an old lady's purse in their thieving little paws. They do no work and yet have unreasonable expectations of others, have pretensions to brilliance but are insipid, and routinely express their disdain with an air of sanctimonious condescension. While it is a fair observation that many humans share all of these unhandsome qualities, those people do not also defecate in a box in my home.

Lucy the Desert Cat was saved from drowning in a swimming pool in California, which prompted Hannah to observe that, since the kitten was such a poor swimmer, it would be a good idea to bring her to Nevada, where there is so little water. This is the kind of logic fathers must deal with regularly, and, instead of trying to muster a counterargument that makes sense to a kid, we dads soon learn that it is easier just to crack another beer and play along. Although satisfying in the short run, this coping strategy has the long-term consequence that one day, while changing the cat box or cleaning the fishbowl, you realize, suddenly, that kid logic has thoroughly reshaped your life, one kitten and goldfish at a time.

So Lucy joined us here in the high desert of northwestern Nevada, where she promptly received the unearned surname "the Desert Cat," and where she has consistently displayed all the appalling qualities universal to cats, plus other bad behaviors so idiosyncratic as to defy explanation. Like many cats, she scratches the furniture, craps in the houseplants, gets cranked up on catnip, and cools herself down by lapping up toilet water. I defy you to contemplate tolerating this behavior in a person, let alone describing it as "cute." Just try it: "Honey, I invited Sarah over for lunch. She'll shred the couch, poop in the potted palm, get high as a kite, race around the room, and then stick her face in the toilet. She's so *cute!*" Other behaviors are more weird than objectionable. For example, when I agreed to adopt the cat, I rationalized that I could use a good mouser. But while Lucy is content to nap as mice run circles around her, she is fiercely devoted to hunting fence lizards, whose bloody, tailless, still-wriggling carcasses she delivers to the living room carpet whenever she isn't counting mice through half-shut eyes.

Then there's Lucy's peculiar arboreal habit. Hannah and Caroline like to gather sticks and build nests in juniper trees in the hope that birds will inhabit them—a neat trick that on one memorable occasion actually worked. The problem is that the cat climbs the trees and sits in the nests but knows as much about getting out of a tree as she does about laying an egg. Then, there's the unconscionable way she treats my flatulent old dog, who, like me, simply wants to be left in peace to daydream and listen to baseball on the radio. Lucy likes to visit Darcy as she naps, nuzzle her affectionately, then slap her on the snout with her paw, curl around, and stick her ass in the dog's face—all before slinking away to knock over a liquor store. Worst of all is our cat's bizarre habit of walking across my keyboard as I am writing, which she does in a regular rhythm that usually results in the cryptic three-paw cluster of "dfc…7yu…p[,." Even if this is more eloquent than some of what I come up with on my own, I still find it irritating.

The worst thing about the cat is that the trouble she causes leads to "solutions" far worse than the problems they are intended to solve. When the cat took up strutting on the counters, for example, we resorted to a high-tech remedy: cans of compressed air equipped with whistling, motion-sensing nozzles. The result is that Lucy has learned how to slalom the counters without triggering the devices, while I routinely come in from work, forget that the cat blasters are set to detonate, and end up having to change my underwear before I pour my first whiskey.

The ancient Egyptians worshipped cats, which they called "mau," believing the animals to be magical protectors, and even going so far as to mummify some. Lucy's remarkable powers of self-preservation cause me to wonder if there may be something to this myth. When she was a kitten, Lucy could have been eaten by just about any critter out here, from red tails and bobcats to harriers and mountain lions. Even an adult cat should fear the odds here, where the most active predators of small mammals are coyotes, golden eagles, and great horned owls. Old Man Coyote alone can eat several rabbits a day (and what is a cat, finally, but just a sort of lazy, pampered rabbit?), and you need only listen to the wonderful call-and-response howling of coyote bands at night to do the math and conclude that there is a lot of skull crunching going on out there amid the beauty of balsamroot and lupine. Despite these many threats, Lucy the Desert Cat abides.

This cat's terrible habits and magical ability to elude predators have prompted me to think more about other kinds of accidents that might befall her on Ranting Hill. For example, she always hangs around when I am trenching with the backhoe, a situation in which pushing a lever one way rather than the other would forever rid me of cat blasters but also break my daughters' hearts. Lucy also stays fairly close when I'm bucking logs, and a chainsaw is especially hazardous when wielded by a man distracted by the looming chore of cleaning the cat box. Most gratifying is the contemplation of what the weed-whacker might accomplish if swung suddenly catward at full throttle. While such a mishap would address the problem of my toilet being used as a drinking vessel, it would certainly result in my family voting me off Ranting Hill, where I would then have no toilet at all—not that I relieve myself indoors very often in any case.

The distribution of power in my family ensures that Lucy the Desert Cat will remain safe and sound, perhaps soon to be rewarded for her "cuteness" with the privilege of driving my truck to town to buy catnip and expensive rye with my credit card. Speaking as a father who has officiated a funeral ceremony for a goldfish, I think it unlikely I will succeed in relegating Lucy to the garage, much less having the opportunity to fire up the Stihl and buck her into furry little rounds. No, my fate was sealed long ago, perhaps even before I received the transformative news that our first daughter was preparing to enter this beautiful world. The way I reckon it, though, 95 percent blessing is a respectable stat, even if it does cause some dfc...7yu...p[,.

HOW MANY BARS IN YOUR CELL?

T HE RURAL POCKET of Silver Hills where we live is so re- mote as to be virtually uninhabited, and I am delighted to be among its virtual uninhabitants. This status comes with some logistical challenges, though: roads that are often impassable, the real threat of wildfire, long response times for emergency services, and the risk that a tragic miscalculation might cause a person to run out of beer during the World Series. The most interesting liability of our isolation, however, is that the cell phone companies are unsure if we exist. Their coverage map for our area looks like a Great Basin gopher snake: a long, slim, sinuous band of human contact wriggling through a vast desert of incommunicado wildlands. Out here on the frontier of digital Terra Incognita we are barely on the map. This liminal status has never bothered me, and since our move out to this big country from town I have missed almost nothing I've lost and have treasured almost everything I have gained. Whenever I am asked why I choose to live in the middle of nowhere, I'm reminded that, from my point of view, I have the privilege of living in the middle of everywhere.

One practical problem with being a virtual uninhabitant of the middle of everywhere is that it is an easy place to pull an Everett Ruess or Chris McCandless—to go out for a stroll and simply vanish into the vast labyrinth of unnamed hills and canyons that extend west from here to California. For this reason, my wife—in acknowledgment of my charm, wit, and habit of bringing home a paycheck—thought it best to ensure my safety by getting me a smartphone to carry out into the wilderness. Because I average around 1,300 miles of solo walking in these wildlands each year, she reckoned that at some point the odds could catch up with me, in which case I might want to just sit in the sage and call a relief helicopter to medivac me back to the world of bourbon and baseball.

When I protested my looming enphonement—not because I'm a Luddite purist but, rather, because I'm exceedingly stubborn and cheap—my wife mentioned my paternal obligations, which rendered further resistance futile. Besides, I rationalized, a smartphone might be handy out there in case of a real emergency, like remembering that I failed to put a fresh box of IPA into my beer fridge before setting out on a long hike.

So Eryn stuck me with the fancy phone, and off I went, back into the wilderness, where, after a series of methodical trials, I discovered that the phone has reception in one spot and one spot only: the very peak of our local mountain, about five miles from home and 2,000 feet above it. In effect, there was only one place where I could afford to have an accident—though, in fairness, it was a good place, and I could easily imagine heroically clasping the swinging rope ladder as the chopper plucked me off the east face of the mountain's sheer granite palisades. Nevertheless, the reality is that the near-total lack of coverage makes the phone useless, and until pronghorn and coyotes start texting there is no profit margin in pointing a satellite at me out there.

But here is the strange part: Before getting the smartphone, I rarely contemplated the real risks I run in this wild place; now, because I have the phone and know it won't work, I worry that this unreliable piece of emergency equipment will leave me vulnerable to fires and snakebite, driving snow and freezing winds, dehydration and heat stroke. Before acquiring the phone, I was a blithely happy eccentric walking around alone in the desert; since getting it, I have become a fretting eccentric walking around alone in the desert obsessing that he won't be able to count on his phone to save him.

On the other hand, carrying a piece of emergency equipment that I am certain cannot help me has profoundly altered the way I think about the thousands of miles I walk out in the Silver Hills. Rather than harboring a cavalier, unexamined assumption of my own invulnerability, I feel humbled, and in that humility I have become more vigilant. I now routinely carry a hefty daypack with extra food, water, and clothes, and I take the compass, headlamp, and bivvy sack. I check the weather before I head out, and I think more carefully than ever about elevation, hydration, and exposure. I notice the direction of the wind, or a sudden drop in temperature, or the behavior of wild animals when a storm is brewing.

Maybe Emerson was onto something when he observed that civilized man "has a fine Geneva watch, but he fails of the skill to tell the hour by the sun." My cell phone was my fancy watch, but because I knew that I could not rely upon it, I watched the angle of the sun more carefully than ever before, and in this new habit of attention I became, as Uncle Waldo himself put it, self-reliant. In a strange way, my worthless phone had helped me to escape some small prison of dependency. Over time, I also found that I enjoyed a more profound sense of my own isolation. I was utterly alone out there, and I knew that not because I had no phone but because I had a phone with which I could not possibly contact another human being. It was a sweet liberation to feel the modest rectangular bump in my pocket and be reminded that I am, just as I want to be, entirely out of touch.

While it is easy to wax rhapsodic about the ennobling virtues of my useless phone, I confess that I often find myself contemplating what purposes it might serve if the worst were to happen—if I were to be incapacitated in the wild by blizzard or wildfire or buzzworm venom. Just as a broken clock is nevertheless correct twice each day, I have reason to suspect that my useless phone might somehow prove handy in an emergency. While I could not call for help, maybe I could use the phone to dig, like a pawing coyote, through the sand in search of life-preserving water. Would it work to strike it against granite to spark a fire? Or, maybe I could use it as Cactus Ed Abbey used his rock in *Desert Solitaire*, to bean a harmless jackrabbit and thus keep myself alive another day or two? Or, perhaps I could get a glint off the screen sufficient to improvise a signal mirror, alerting rescuers to my remote location. And if, after all, it did *not* work to use the phone to secure water, fire, food, or salvation, at least I could, after bashing my fist against a boulder in a fit of helpless frustration, use it as a splint to brace my fractured wrist.

Even in a case so dire that my phone did nothing to aid my survival, it might at least allow me to orchestrate and record my demise. For example, I could use it to play soothing music—say, Bessie Smith crooning "Nobody Knows You When You're Down and Out"; or, perhaps, something nostalgic and pastoral from my lost youth, like John Denver's "Take Me Home, Country Roads"; or maybe something more folksy and Western, like Roy Rogers crooning "Bury Me Not on the Lone Prairie." If the phone had not been repurposed as a splint, I could use it to take a picture of myself—perhaps looking manly and stoical, like Kit Carson or Jim Bridger. Or maybe I'd just go out cool, flashing a peace sign as my final gesture.

I could, instead, create a text message that, although it could not be sent, would later be discovered and allow me to shape my own legacy. I would want something profound, of course. All Henry David Thoreau came up with for last words was "moose . . . Indian," which set the bar for expiring environmental writers mercifully low. (By the way, Thoreau's penultimate words were far better than his final words; when asked if he had made his peace with God, he replied, "I was not aware that we had quarreled.") But I hold with my patron saint, Mark Twain, who insisted that no one should leave something as important as their final words to the last minute. He wisely admonished that preparing in advance enables a person "to say something smart with his latest gasp." I have taken Twain's advice to heart and, after a great deal of consideration, have resolved upon texting these poignant and incisive final words: "crawling 2k ft up mtn 2 call fr hlp—pls put IPA in fridge."

A VISIT FROM THE
MARY KAY LADY

IT IS UNFORTUNATE that we English speakers have relatively few words for *mud*, a substance that varies so greatly by location and conditions that it would be handier to have a hundred terms for it, as the indigenous Nordic Sami people do for *snow*. If a useless neologism like *ginormous* can make the *Oxford English Dictionary*, you would think we could spare an extra word or two to distinguish one person's home mud from another's. Out here in Silver Hills, our mud is less a description of the ground than it is a full season, a marker of identity, and a way of life.

Lacking a hundred helpful synonyms for mud, I think, instead, of stories that suggest what is special about the thick, deep, slippery gunk that we Silver Hillbillies call "gumbo." When hiking during mud season in spring, the gumbo becomes so heavy on our boots that we often find it easier to shuffle along like cross-country skiers than to lift our heavy feet off the ground. When driving on even the slightest slope, it makes little difference whether you put your foot on the gas or the brake, since even while braking you simply slide along without resistance, like a capsule gliding through space. Our gumbo also has the unique quality of sticking to itself, gathering so thickly on truck tires that it is limited only by the wheel wells, which shear it off with each revolution, neat as a spindle turning on a lathe.

In early spring, the road to our house is sometimes so thick with gumbo that it becomes impassible even to high-clearance, four-wheel-drive vehicles. When that happens, we have two choices: park at the paved road and slog several miles through the muck; or, wait until evening, when the mud freezes up, making it viscous enough that it becomes possible to pilot perilously across it. In more than a decade out here, I have never completed a full mud season without sliding off the road, and our family now runs a "gumbo pool": five bucks buys a guess as to the first date on which one of us, neighbors included, will end up in the ditch.

But the best thing about mud season in Silver Hills is the "gumbo luge," which Hannah and Caroline love. Here's how it works. When the spring thaw begins, the first dozen truck trips down our road leave shallow wheel ruts. Those ruts deepen a little each day and by mid-season are so deep that it is risky to try to avoid them, since a slide into the ruts results in a jaw-rattling drop that is hard on spines as well as transmissions. Instead, the trick is to get squarely into these twin tire canyons from the start, after which the impressive depth of the channels unfailingly prevents the vehicle from sliding off the road. In fact, the ruts are so deep that you can drive our road without ever placing your hands on the steering wheel. Instead, you simply slide along, secure in the deep tracks that guide your rig even around hairpin turns. No true Silver Hillbilly would be caught with their hands on the wheel while running the gumbo luge, and it is common practice to lace your fingers behind your head while gunning your truck along through the muddy slots.

One morning, during the height of mud season, I was sitting at my writing desk and looking out the window—which is about all I do at my writing desk—when I saw a spectacle so astonishing and surreal that I grabbed my birding binoculars to scope it out. There, in the twin tubes of the binocs, was a pink Cadillac, fishtailing wildly up our driveway. Understand that in all my years on Ranting Hill, I had never seen a two-wheel-drive vehicle out here during mud season, that our driveway is an unbroken half-mile long sheet of hazardous gumbo, and that the only pink things I have ever seen around here are rock penstemon, long-leafed phlox, and my kids' pacifiers. I instantly sprinted for the door, booted up, and headed out to see what would become of whomever was crazy enough to brave Silver Hills gumbo in a Caddy.

From the crest of the knoll beneath Ranting Hill I witnessed an utterly indelible image: the pink Cadillac had gone sideways off the driveway, slid down a small hill, and lodged firmly atop a charred juniper stump, where it rested with its rear end up in the air and its wheels spinning madly, shotgunning mud everywhere. Covering my face with my forearm to deflect the gumbo strafing, I worked my way down to the car, which had music blaring from behind its tinted windows. I rapped on the driver's side window and waited for a reply. Eventually, the power window rolled slowly down, and Loretta Lynn came blasting out: "*Well, sloe gin fizz works mighty fast, when you drink it by the pitcher and not by the glass!*" In the driver's seat was a middle-aged woman who looked uncannily like Loretta, only frosted blonde. She held in her hand a highball glass, from which she had apparently managed to spill not one drop of her cocktail. Rather than turning the music down, she held her pointer finger up, as if to say, "hold on a second," then took a sip of her drink and gunned the engine again.

"Your tires aren't on the ground!" I shouted over the cranking tunes, revving engine, and splattering mud.

"What's that, hon?" she yelled back.

"*Your tires!*" I screamed, pointing helpfully toward the part of her car that was three feet off the ground.

She took another sip of her cocktail, leaned slowly out the window, craned her neck backward, and then began to laugh, reaching out to give me a fist bump, as if she had just slapped in the game-winning RBI. She then turned off the ignition and, in the silence that followed, said in a gravelly voice, "I'm the Mary Kay lady. Want a drink?"

If she looked like Loretta Lynn, she sounded more like Tom Waits. Though it was eleven in the morning, I felt obliged not to let her drink alone, and so I promptly agreed. She spread her knees, reached down between her ankles, and pulled a thermos and second highball glass from beneath the driver's seat, pouring me a tall one of something that tasted suspiciously like straight gin.

"I came to invite you to a party," she said, "but I forgot the invitation. I don't want to get my heels muddy," she continued, pulling out her phone, "so let's just have a drink." She made a quick call, described roughly where she was, and instructed someone on the other end of the line to "bring blush."

We passed the next half hour pleasantly, she turning the Loretta back on and passing fresh drinks through the window, me standing up to my ankles in gumbo and receiving what I am guessing were excellent tips about skin care. Just as we polished off the thermos, a large man wearing a huge hat came riding up the driveway on a ginormous horse. He dismounted with a wide smile, climbed down the hill, shook my hand firmly, then lifted the Mary Kay lady out through the window of the Caddy, drink still in hand, gently folding her over his broad shoulder like a sack of grain. Clambering up the slope, he placed her on the horse, whose name, it turned out, was Blush. He then slid the pointed toe of his boot into the stirrup and swung himself up behind her, encircling her waist with his arms, as the two of them rode off together, laughing. I could see her clear plastic heels tapping Blush's flanks, as the big man hollered back at me, "Thanks, chief. See ya after mud season!"

It took a few weeks for the gumbo to firm up enough for a tow truck to get in and winch out the abandoned car, during which time I had the great pleasure of sitting at my writing desk, looking out at that beautiful pink wreck stranded down there among the gooseberry and rabbitbrush. To commemorate the visit from the Mary Kay lady, whose name I never learned, I did what I think any eccentric, reclusive writer would have done: I composed a haiku.

Light pink Cadillac
High-centered on an old stump
Wheels spinning freely.

THE WASHOE ZEPHYR

T HOSE OF US WHO LIVE in these high desert foothills are all too familiar with the summer wind that is known locally as the Washoe Zephyr. During his time as a cub newspaper reporter in the mining camps of the western Nevada Territory (then nicknamed "Washoe," after the native people who inhabit the eastern foothills of the Sierra Nevada), Mark Twain was also familiar with this special wind, which was already the stuff of tall tales by the time he arrived on the Comstock in the early 1860s. Calling the Washoe Zephyr "a soaring dust-drift about the size of the United States set up edgewise," in *Roughing It* (1872) Twain described the layers of items he observed blowing by above him: "hats, chickens, and parasols sailing in the remote heavens; blankets, tin signs, sagebrush, and shingles a shade lower; door-mats and buffalo-robes lower still; shovels and coal-scuttles on the next grade; glass doors, cats, and little children on the next; disrupted lumber yards, light buggies, and wheelbarrows on the next; and down only thirty or forty feet above ground was a scurrying storm of emigrating roofs and vacant lots." "A Washoe wind," Twain concluded, "is by no means a trifling matter."

Twain's comic exaggeration is funny only if you do not actually live here. In our decade on Ranting Hill, quite a few of the items on Twain's list actually have blown away from here, along with plenty of things he did not think to mention. The Washoe Zephyr hauls off papers and magazines, hats and sweaters, tarps and blankets, but would you believe that it also blows away plastic coolers, bird netting, chicken wire, and five-gallon buckets, that it routinely rolls everything from soccer balls to trash cans off our hill, and that the only way to keep a half-full bottle of beer from being knocked over is to down it straightaway? Our heavy outdoor furniture routinely slides around the patio as if it were an ice rink, and the Zephyr has even toppled well-stacked cords of juniper and pine. Around here the tumbleweed (Russian thistle) does not tumble at all. It is instead dislodged by dust devils, sucked up into the gyre, and transported aloft toward Utah. On one memorable occasion, a sudden blast knifed under the girls' blue, plastic wading pool. I stood, gripping my beer as I watched the cobalt disc simply sail off into the desert sky. It took me an hour of hiking around even to find the pool, which had returned to earth and lodged in a juniper copse a half mile from the house.

Meteorologists call the Washoe Zephyr a seasonal, diurnal wind, because it occurs regularly during the summer and is driven by temperature and pressure gradients that are built up and broken down over the course of the day. Like everything and everybody around here, though, our wind is extremely weird. In the normal pattern, diurnal, mountain-slope winds move upslope during the day and downslope at night—just as you would expect, given that hot air rises and cool air sinks. But here, in the western Great Basin, the pattern is reversed: the wind howls *down* from the canyons all afternoon at twenty to thirty miles per hour, finally shutting off or gently reversing itself an hour or so after dark. What causes this odd wind pattern?

Weather geeks have been arguing about the mechanism of the Washoe Zephyr for a long time. While a number of theories have been proposed, the most persuasive is that this unfailing west-southwest afternoon wind is a "thermally driven flow phenomenon." During the day, heated air rises from the desert floor, creating a conveyor or chimney effect that sucks the cooler air down out of the Sierra Nevada. But the situation is more complicated than that, since the Zephyr is produced not only by this thermal differential but also by a giant, regional-scale pressure gradient. In summer, the low-pressure system produced in the desert of central Nevada remains in an unstable relationship with the high-pressure system formed on the western side of the Sierra. The great equalizer is the Zephyr, which relieves the pressure of this atmospheric asymmetry by pulling California air through the mountain passes and down into the Nevada desert.

Scientific theories notwithstanding, the Zephyr remains a distinctive but poorly understood feature of life in the western Great Basin. Even Twain recognized the mystery surrounding the wind's origin. The Washoe Zephyr, he wrote, is "a peculiarly Scriptural wind, in that no man knoweth 'whence it cometh'. That is to say, where it originates. It comes right over the mountains from the West, but when one crosses the ridge he does not find any of it on the other side!" Like the cloud that often hovers atop Mount Shasta even when skies surrounding the peak are clear, our home wind is produced by the mountains. While we tend to think of wind as something that blows in from somewhere else, the Washoe Zephyr is endemic, a signature phenomenon created by the daily conversation taking place between mountains and desert.

I would need to be pretty softhearted to have much good to say about the Washoe Zephyr, which is more akin to an existential trial than it is to a welcome breeze. A nature writer such as Annie Dillard can emote about the "spiritual energy of wind" only because she is lolling in the gentle breeze that ripples the verdant banks of Virginia's Tinker Creek. As Twain knew so well, the case is entirely different in the Western desert. Here the wind is so desiccating as to make gardening virtually impossible. It is so hot that facing into it is like standing in front of the open door of a kiln being vented into your face by the world's largest exhaust fan. When wildfires burn up in the Sierra, which they do much of each summer, the Zephyr funnels their choking smoke and ash directly into these desert basins and has, on occasion, driven roaring flames toward our home.

Because the Washoe Zephyr shotguns so much desert sand, we must sometimes resort to wearing ski goggles while hiking. Without them, the amount of dirt that ends up in your eyes after a hike would be enough to pot a houseplant with, if your stinging eyeballs were not so dried out as to cause the debris to stick to them almost indefinitely. Inside your boots, you will discover enough gravel to sandbag a levee. And don't bother clenching your teeth in frustration while being blasted by the Zephyr, because you will be doubly exasperated when you feel the grit between your molars. Is it any wonder that the Buddhist and Hindu concept of *nirvana*—which signifies a liberation after a lengthy period of suffering—is understood by some etymologists of Sanskrit to mean a state of *no wind*? Each evening when the blast of the Washoe Zephyr subsides, it is as if the world has suddenly stopped clenching its muscles and squinting its eyes. Calm comes over the land in a form that can never be produced by the absence of wind, but only by a cessation of it.

What has somehow been lost in the story of the Washoe Zephyr is that the name of this big wind is, in fact, a joke—one that originated with Twain and the frontier storytellers he gulped red eye with up in Virginia City. Named for Zephyrus, the Greek god who was celebrated as the bringer of light summer breezes, the word *zephyr* specifically evokes the gentle stirring of a soft, Western breeze. This is what Shakespeare intended, when, in *Cymbeline*, he wrote that two beautiful children "Are as gentle / as zephyrs blowing below the violet, / Not wagging his sweet head." Calling our ripping Washoe wind a *zephyr* is a triumph of the sort of ironic understatement that is essential to the American tall-tale tradition. The droll implication of the Washoe Zephyr's name is that out here in the desert West the landscape is so vast and intense that our version of a gentle breeze is a blast that carries off lumber yards, wheelbarrows, children, and vacant lots.

We desert rats do not enjoy the Zephyr, but we endure it, and in enduring it we are made more thoroughly a part of this place. That the name of this grueling, incessant wind is a wry joke is very much to the point. We also endure the desert through laughter, which seems a fit gesture of reciprocation with a landscape that so often seems to be laughing at us—that chuckles knowingly even at our vain pretention to inhabit it. But if the Washoe Zephyr were suddenly to cease forever, a fleeting moment of nirvana might be followed by a sense that something extraordinary had vanished from this land. Because our embrace of nature in this place is an expression of struggle as well as affection, the Washoe Zephyr is something we can no longer live without.

BALLOONS ON THE MOON

O UR PART OF THE DESERT West is so inaccessible that the
common detritus of the dominant endemic species, *Hillbilli-
cus nevadensis redneckii,* is nowhere to be seen. So while the rutted,
dusty BLM roads in the sandy, sage-choked wash bottoms are be-
ribboned with spent shell casings, wide-mouthed bottles of Coors
light, and empty cans of chew, there is simply no easy way to litter
the steep, rocky high country. However, there is one unfortunate
exception to this rule, and that is when trash is airlifted into these
isolated mountains and canyons in the form of balloons.

I have picked up so many trashed balloons over the years that
I find myself wondering what the hell is so jolly about California, which is the nearby, upwind place where all this aerial trash
originates. Maybe the prevalence of balloons in the otherwise
litter-free high desert should not surprise me, since millions of
balloons are released in the United States each year. We release
balloons at graduation celebrations, birthday parties, wedding ceremonies, football games, even funerals. There is actually a company

called Eternal Ascent that will, for fifteen hundred dollars, load your ashes into a balloon and float them away. Balloon launches for a pet's ashes cost only six hundred dollars, though, so if I go this route, I have instructed my family to claim I was a Saint Bernard.

The moment a balloon is released it becomes trash, and this trash can cover serious ground. A sixteen-inch-diameter, helium-filled latex toy balloon will float for twenty-four to thirty-six hours and can cover hundreds of miles while climbing to an altitude of 25,000 feet, where it freezes, explodes, and rains down to earth in the form of garbage, which some desert rat like me then has to tote home in his backpack. And while latex balloons will, eventually, biodegrade, the same is not true of metalized nylon balloons, which become a permanent feature of the natural environment. That is the downside of these so-called foil balloons; their only upside is that they are *really shiny*.

Because they conduct electricity, metalized balloons also cause hundreds of blackouts in the United States each year by short-circuiting power lines, which de facto suggests the vulnerability of the grid. If Edward Abbey or Barry Commoner were alive today, they might enjoy the idea that the elaborate infrastructure of postindustrial capitalism can be brought down by a single, drifting, metalized Mickey Mouse. So the next time you release a balloon, do not think of it as a celebratory symbol of freedom. Think of it as trash. You should also think of it as you would a message in a bottle, because someday, somewhere, there is a chance that someone like me will have to read whatever unimaginative nonsense is on your balloon. Given this rare opportunity to communicate across time and space, please try to come up with something more clever than the message on the frog-shaped foil balloon I recovered out here yesterday: "Hoppy Birthday."

By now, you may be wondering what kind of dark-souled curmudgeon would go out of his way to profess loathing for the universally beloved balloon. I confess that I am taking this principled stand against balloons in part because I would otherwise need to stand against something harder to fight, like corporate greed or global climate change. But there is one use of balloons that I approve of wholeheartedly: to make one's lawn chair fly. Manned balloon flights date back to the early eighteenth century, but when Mark Twain defined a balloon as a "thing to take meteoric observations and commit suicide with," he anticipated the incredible adventure of a true Western American folk hero, "Lawnchair Larry."

Truck driver Larry Walters was a man with a dream. On July 2, 1982, in a backyard in suburban San Pedro, California, Larry tied forty-two large, helium-filled balloons to his aluminum lawn chair, which he dubbed *Inspiration I*. He then outfitted the lawn chair with the same gear that Western heroes have always provisioned themselves with: sandwiches, beer, and a gun. But Larry had made a serious miscalculation, and when his friends cut the cord that tethered him to California, he disappeared in a meteoric rise of more than 1,000 feet per minute. Larry did not level out until he reached an altitude of almost 16,000 feet, where he drifted into LAX's airspace and was spotted by a TWA pilot, who found himself reporting to air traffic control that he had just seen a gun-toting guy in a lawn chair sail by. Larry managed to shoot a few of his balloons before accidentally dropping his pellet gun, after which he descended slowly into a Long Beach neighborhood, where he became entangled in power lines and caused a twenty-minute blackout. Perfectly unharmed, he climbed down from his lawn chair and was immediately arrested. When a reporter asked about the inspiration for his epic, fourteen-hour flight, Larry replied, "A man can't just sit around."

Larry's heroic adventure notwithstanding, the fact remains that unless you want to fly in a lawn chair or take down the power grid, balloons are trash. Fun trash. Colorful trash. But trash just the same. Now, the problem with being both an environmentalist and a father is that whenever I rant about an issue I always end up caught by my daughters in some act of complicity that exposes my hypocrisy. In this case, the trouble started when little Caroline insisted that we celebrate sister Hannah's ninth birthday with a balloon release. I was in a tough spot, since I had to choose between being an uptight, sanctimonious, balloon-reviling ecogeek and being a really cool dad who happened to be externalizing the true cost of his coolness by exporting some aerial trash downwind to Utah. I remained on the fence, until Caroline explained that our balloons would not go to Utah but rather to the moon, where she intended to clean them up herself, just as soon as she becomes an astronaut.

Well, that was pretty persuasive, so we began preparations for our birthday launch. We would use latex rather than Mylar, we would release only one balloon per kid, and we would be careful to aim them at the moon. We also decided that, just in case they ended up on the other side of the Great Basin—in the Wasatch Mountains instead of the lunar mountains—we would write something witty on the balloons to help compensate the finder for their trouble. On one balloon we wrote, "PLEASE RETURN TO LARRY WALTERS." On the other, "SORRY, UTAH!" We then ate some birthday cake and ice cream before heading outside to position ourselves for the launch. The girls aimed for the moon, I counted down from ten to blastoff, and they opened their small hands and sent the bright yellow and orange balloons on their way into the azure Nevada sky. The balloons rose, the girls cheered, the moon waited. It was one of those sparkling experiences when time, worry, and even the desert wind—everything in the world, save two rising balloons—stood still for one long, gorgeous moment.

I try to tell myself that, because I have retrieved more than a hundred trashed balloons from the remote desert, I have earned the right to release a few, but I know that is just more of the same evasive horseshit we all tell ourselves every day. The plain fact is that I littered, and that I had a lot of fun doing it. I hope my neighbors in Utah will cut me some slack on this one. After all, a man can't just sit around.

GUESTS IN THE
HOUSE OF FIRE

F IRE HAS REMAINED ABSENT from our home landscape this
summer, at least so far. Winter was so long and wet as to have
delayed fire season, and it seems strange that our home mountain,
valley, and foothills have remained unscorched even into mid-
summer. After so many years of scrutinizing weather—of spend-
ing July and August with a beer in one hand and binoculars in the
other, of phoning in plumes every month or so—there is something
almost disconcerting about this lack of fire. This fireless summer has
made me feel like the urbanite who flees to the country to escape the
constant din of the city and then can't sleep because it is too quiet.
After all, this land was sculpted by burning, the natural fire cycle
here having been as short as fifteen years. Wildfires are common,
and their fuel is as much the intense aridity and desiccating wind as
it is the sage, rabbitbrush, and bitterbrush, the juniper, gooseberry,
and desert peach. Out here, fire isn't an accident; it's weather.

Last July, a simultaneous trio of wind-driven wildfires burned
more than 12,000 acres of our home mountain and valley,

prompting evacuations along the wildlands interface where we live. The first two nights of the fire, which for their safety Eryn and the girls spent in town, proved relatively uneventful. I was fortunate to have a crew of wildlands firefighters occupying our two main firebreaks, and I spent those nights bringing them coffee and listening to their incredible stories about the unpredictable power of fire. Even as the glowing clouds of smoke in the Western sky reflected the flames marching up the valley on the other side of the foothills, I remained fairly confident that my defensible space and fuels reduction work would make it possible for these guys to save our house, even if the fire ultimately crested Ranting Hill.

By afternoon on the third day, however, things were worse. The fire had moved closer and was burning hotter, and the winds had intensified. Visibility was radically reduced by the thickening smoke, which was now heavy with ash lifted from the incineration of the sagebrush steppe out on the public lands. The acrid smoke stung my eyes and burned in my nostrils and throat, even though I had adopted the precaution of tying a bandana over my face, train-robber style. Then, about two hours before dark, an arm of the blaze to our north jumped a firebreak on the BLM and threatened more homes, resulting in the hurried redeployment of the crews protecting our place. I will never forget my feeling of exhaustion and anxiety as I watched those brush trucks and water tenders roll away. Left alone at the house, I had no choice but to watch and wait.

At dusk, just as the smoky darkness began to settle and the sky faintly resumed its fiery glow, the wind suddenly shifted. I knew immediately I was in trouble—that there were no longer any crews between me and the fire and that the scalding winds would funnel the flames through the canyon gaps toward our home. I raced out onto the balcony, faced directly into the warm wind, and raised my binoculars to scope the western horizon. In the foreground of my field of vision was my neighbor's house and barn; in the distance was open sagebrush steppe spread out beneath a toothed ridgeline that was chiseled into the falling sky. As I scanned that ridge through the binocs, a half-mile-long curtain of flames suddenly broke over it like a wave, cresting the horizon and pushing forward in a wind-driven phalanx that seemed to suck the air out of my chest. In almost the same moment, I spun around to see an immense, red-bellied, firefighting air tanker coming at me out of the thick smoke. Flying over our roof, it seemed impossibly large and dangerously low. As it roared above me I watched it drop yet lower, over my neighbor's house, releasing, as it did, several thousand gallons of water and fire retardant, colored fuchsia by its ferris oxide. It was a surreal moment: the darkness falling and the smoke swirling, the sky glowing and the fire blazing in an approaching wall, and then the immense cloud of bright-pink retardant cascading across the juniper-dotted desert. That was the last image I registered before scrambling off the balcony, jumping into my truck, and racing to town by a circuitous backcountry route that reduced the chance of fire blocking my escape. One glimpse of that wall of flames had convinced me that I would have nothing to say about what this fire ultimately did.

From town, we scoured the news for clues about what might be happening in the wildlands surrounding Ranting Hill, but information was frustratingly slow and imprecise. We knew all the roads were closed now, and things were bad. Beyond that, there was no way to tell what might be going on.

Early the next morning, when it was declared safe, my dad and I drove out to the house, saying little and not knowing what we would find. The beautiful culmination of our family's many years of saving, planning, and work might still be standing—or it might not. Arriving in our rural neighborhood, we soon learned that fire crews had been redeployed to our road just in time; although several of my neighbors' fences burned, none of us lost a home.

It is true that we came to this wild place to be exposed to the power of forces beyond our control, including wind, snow, aridity, and even fire. That fuchsia stain on the desert remained visible for several years, a humbling reminder that we desert rats remain guests in the house of fire. Even now, when I come home tired from a long day at work, I am sometimes able to see our house the way I saw it that morning: with a kind of inspired surprise that keeps fresh my deep appreciation for the special place that is our home.

IN DEFENSE OF BIBLIOPEDESTRIANISM

I FREELY ADMIT that those of us who live in remote desert places tend to be eccentric, though it remains unclear to me whether the weird are attracted to this wild country or if our weirdness is instead produced by it. When you live in relative isolation—and in a severe physical environment that conspires with that isolation to scour away affectation and superfluity—you discover some odd things about yourself, among which is that you are odd. Living in this high desert outback also helps correct for the homogenizing tendencies of living in town, where our unique character is too easily distorted or diluted by the social demands of conformity, consistency, and compromise. Out here, we tend to revert to whatever we might have been if the demands of the social contract had never been imposed on us in the first place. I do not claim that the end result of this process is always pretty. On the contrary, neither nature nor human nature inspires much romanticism out here, where a pastoral fantasy is about as sustainable as an orchid in the desert sun. Still, it is liberating to live in a place where no one is close enough to see what you are up to, let alone volunteer their opinion that you ought to mow your lawn or go to church.

A recitation of my own weird habits and tendencies would be lengthy. And while I am not in the habit of expounding upon these innumerable idiosyncrasies, Hannah has reached an age at which she has begun to insist that I explain and defend them—an exercise that largely defeats the purpose of rural desert living, in which the sanctity of indefensible eccentricity is all but holy. As it turns out, however, this concept of freedom is too abstract for Hannah, whose social comparisons have led her to the mildly troubling conclusion that I am "totally not like other dads."

As Hannah becomes more socially aware, more concerned about what is normal, and more worried that our family may not qualify, I am barraged with unanswerable questions. Why do I correct the baseball radio announcers when I know they can't hear me? Why do I tell chicken-crossing-the-road jokes to our laying hens? Why am I not afraid of scorpions and rattlesnakes but nervous around cows? Why do I fly kites using a fishing pole? How did I ever learn so much about pronghorn antelope without learning *anything* about her favorite pop stars? Why do I have pet names for my chainsaw ("Landshark") and weed-whacker ("Cujo")? Why do I always have to say what kind of animal's butt the poop came from? Why do I like to put goldfish into the BLM stock tanks? Why do I so often wear no pants? This kind of interrogation makes me wish my kid would just ask about something simple, like mortality, God, or where babies come from. But, no, it always has to be the "no pants thing" again.

Recently, Hannah lighted on a new "Daddy is so weird" behavior, which she asked me to defend: "Dad, why do you read while you walk?" Reading while I hike through the desert is a habit I developed so long ago that it never occurred to me that it might require explanation. I could have replied, "Because I walk about

1,300 miles a year around here, I get bored," but while I do walk that much, I never lose interest in this landscape. I could have said, "I have a lot of work to do and can't afford the time to hike unless I'm also reading," but that's not quite true either. I might have pointed out, "I'm no weirder than the knotheads you see walking around town checking their phones until they bump into each other," but my pride would not allow the comparison. Ultimately, I decided that I should try to give Hannah an honest, helpful answer. To do that, I would first have to scrutinize my odd habit of peripatetic reading.

For starters, walking and reading are two of the most important activities in my life, so perhaps it was inevitable that I would eventually combine them. The two are also similar in many ways. Walking and reading are both forms of exercise: one working out the body, the other the mind. Both are excellent when pursued in solitude. Both get us from one place to another, and yet the main purpose of each is the journey, not the destination. If this were not the case, why would we re-read a beloved book or repeat a favorite hike? Both activities enlarge our sense of the world, expanding the territory and helping us to place ourselves within it. Of the many meanings of the word *walk*, "to go away" has been in use since the mid-fifteenth century. Isn't this precisely what we do while reading? Doesn't a good book, like a good hike, offer a salutary voyage away from home and into a series of challenges and surprises that ultimately gives the concept of home its meaning? Finally, while most of us are capable of both reading and walking, few of us do much of either. Mark Twain is reputed to have observed that "the man who does not read has no advantage over the man who cannot read." I would say the same about a person who has healthy legs but chooses not to walk.

While Karl Marx made some perceptive pronouncements about the value of books, I prefer the insight offered by that wiser

Marx, Groucho, who used to say that "outside of a dog, a book is a man's best friend. Inside of a dog, it's too dark to read." A book, like a dog, is good company, and I do not cotton to heading out to hike without taking both along with me. I also like the contrasts a carefully chosen book can create with the landscape through which I move. There is nothing like being on the Mississippi River with Twain or at sea with Melville or pond-side with Thoreau or along Tinker Creek with Dillard while I am shuffling through the sagebrush and alkali dust. When it gets hot, I love a book like Barry Lopez's *Arctic Dreams* or Rick Bass's *Winter*. When it turns cold and windy, I head to warmer climes in books by Wendell Berry, Gary Nabhan, or Ellen Meloy, or I voyage out to the Hawaiian Islands in the inimitable poetry of W. S. Merwin.

While the cultural dominance of the automobile has profoundly reconditioned our sense of space and time—as when we ask someone how far it is to a place and receive a reply in minutes rather than miles—I like knowing the precise relationship between walking routes and pages. If I intend to read a twenty-page essay, I choose a canyon-bottom stroll that will bring me home just as I am turning the final page; if I prefer to read a novella, I will need enough time to crest the Moonrise and Palisades ridges and loop back around Cow Canyon past the spring.

Even John Muir, who is surely among the most justly celebrated of great walkers, packed books on the trail. On his famous 1867 thousand-mile walk from Indianapolis to the Gulf of Mexico, for example, he carried the New Testament, *Paradise Lost*, and a book of poems by fellow Scottish countryman Robert Burns. Muir was also familiar with the "book of nature," a trope known since the time of Plato but also present in many cultures, both ancient and modern. *Liber naturae*, the book of nature, is the idea that the natural world is a form of sacred text and that the revelation of its divinity is dependent upon our willingness to read it carefully. For theologians of the Latin Middle Ages—and even for Muir—the world of the book and the book of the world were intimately related to each other.

Of course, I am no Plato or Muir, and by temperament I am closer to Groucho than I am to Karl. And this is a wide-open desert with a thousand hazards. It is true that I have, on a number of occasions, read myself into trouble while on the hoof, as when I paused to enjoy an especially engaging Pattiann Rogers poem only to discover that I was standing atop a mound of irate harvester ants. I have also stepped into the tunnels of California ground squirrels, a risk that, for some reason, seems especially acute when I am reading Chuck Bowden or Terry Tempest Williams. Most concerning are the Great Basin rattlers, which maintain a "don't tread on me" (or is it "don't read on me"?) attitude, even if I am enjoying a book by a herpetophile like Cactus Ed Abbey when I come upon them.

But most of the surprises that come from simultaneous reading and hiking are good ones, because looking from the world of nature to the world of the printed page and back again becomes a game of peekaboo: now you don't see it, now you do. Once, I looked up from reading to see a pronghorn buck etched into the ridgeline above me. On another occasion, I glanced up in time to notice a pair of coyote pups, not more than a few weeks old, cross a sandy island in the sagebrush sea. One evening, as it became too dark to make out the page, I lifted my head to witness the thinnest possible crescent moon, in close conjunction with Venus, floating just above the summit ridge of our home mountain.

When we read a travel guidebook while walking in a city or a natural history field guide while hiking through a forest, we are considered normal. It is understood that we need the book to know and name the things of this world and to prevent ourselves from becoming lost within it. As I explained to Hannah, I believe good writing plays the same orienting role: it can help us discover where we are and why our connections to each other and to this world we walk through each day are so precious to begin with. While she still insists that I am totally not like other dads, Hannah's own passion for reading ultimately persuaded her to accept my reasoning.

"Yeah, Dad, I can totally see that. Thanks for taking time to explain it to me," she said. "Now, what about that no pants thing?"

LAWN GUILT

Henry David Thoreau's neighbors generally thought of him as a lazy, confrontational, sanctimonious pain in the ass. They might be interested to know that, on the big issues, he turned out to be right about nearly everything, from his strident support for the abolition of slavery to his scathing exposure of the racial injustice of the Mexican-American War to his embracing of then-new evolutionary theory to his claim that the American relationship to nature was becoming commodified and exploitative. The best example of Thoreau being correct and ahead of his time, however, is offered by his vehement condemnation of the American lawn. In his brilliant 1862 deathbed essay, "Walking," Thoreau wrote, "Hope and the future for me are not in lawns." Instead, he imagined establishing his home on a plot of land covered with wild plants and trees. "Why not put my house—my parlor—behind this plot," he asked, "instead of behind that meager assemblage of curiosities—that poor apology for a Nature and Art, which I call my front yard?"

Calling his neighbors' front yards a "poor apology for a Nature and Art" is the sort of sarcastic face-slapping that was cranky Uncle Henry's specialty, and it is revealing that one of his final utterances before departing this world was a condemnation of lawns. How prescient was he? Riddle: considered acre-for-acre, what is the most pesticide-, herbicide-, water-, labor-, and cash-intensive crop grown in the United States? Right. Your lawn. In America, turf grasses, which are mostly non-native, cover twenty-one million acres (think the state of Maine), cost forty billion dollars per year (more than US foreign aid), consume around ninety million pounds of fertilizer and eighty million pounds of pesticides per year (which sometimes contaminate our groundwater and surface water), and slurp up an inconceivable nine billion gallons of water *per day* (at least half of all residential water use in the arid West is associated with lawns and landscaping).

All this is before we reckon the colossal time suck that lawns represent. Each year, Americans spend an average of three billion hours pushing or (even worse) riding mowers, most of which pollute at a rate ten times that of our cars. In fact, if a lawn were a car, it would be a Hummer: a resource-intensive, plainly unsustainable luxury item that looks cool but is environmentally destructive. As for biodiversity, forget it. Lawns are exotic, barren monocultures. While they are sometimes referred to as "ecological deserts," this characterization is an insult to deserts, which are remarkably biodiverse ecosystems. Consider also the unfortunate symbolic connotations of the lawn. As the food writer Michael Pollan points out, the American lawn is the ultimate manifestation of our culture's perverse fantasy of the total control of nature. As Pollan put it so memorably, "A lawn is nature under totalitarian rule."

Now, hang with me while I descend from my eco-soapbox to offer this surprising confession: I have a lawn. I'm a Westerner. A desert rat. An environmentalist. Even an admirer of Thoreau (though it chaps my hide that he's always right). But I hereby confess to having a lawn. My dual status as arid lands environmentalist and lawn-watering dolt has provoked in me a serious identity crisis, one that reminds me of another of Thoreau's insights (this one, from *Walden*, paraphrasing Matthew 6:3): "Do not let your left hand know what your right hand does." Am I proud of my lawn? Absolutely not. I am completely ashamed of it. I have a terminal case of lawn guilt. But, at the risk of having my membership in the Wilderness Society revoked, it is time to come clean about my immoderate love of the lawn I have planted here on Ranting Hill.

For me, the first challenge is squaring a condition of brutal lawnlessness with fond memories of my suburban childhood, in which the grassy yard provided the most immediate respite from concrete and asphalt. Lawns were our play zones, the part of the vernacular landscape that could be experienced with all our senses, and one of the few suburban spaces not designed specifically to accommodate cars. Even if your old man was on his hands and knees pulling crabgrass every Saturday, for the rest of the week the lawn remained the sovereign province of children—a little patch of freedom that functioned as a clean, green canvas that we kids painted with our imaginative play.

Like a lot of suburban boys, I also experienced the lawn as the first significant site of labor. Before I reached age sixteen and landed my dream job stocking the beer cooler in the local drugstore, the lawn was the only game in town for an enterprising kid who was willing to work hard and needed a little cash. I built a pretty decent side biz as a mower; in this sense the American lawn bought me a new bike, a fishing trip, and tickets to some memorable blues concerts. As I got a bit older, lawn mowing even functioned as my French Foreign Legion. I spent one summer as a mower for a small, under-the-table and off-the-books outfit made up entirely of guys who had been recently dumped by their girlfriends. In fact, having been jilted was a formal requirement of employment with this crew. My mowing partner that summer was a Harley dude named Chaos, who somehow survived on a diet consisting solely of Schlitz beer and corn nuts. Sometimes, Chaos and I would knock out twenty lawns in a day. Between yards, we would crank up the tunes on the battered old truck's cassette deck and lament that we'd been cast away by girls who, we reassured each other, did not have their heads on straight. When I later got my own head on straight and went to college, so revered was the lawn that my school had a world-famous precision lawn-mower brigade that routinely stole the show from reputable marching bands during parades.

Of course, these are memories from another place and time, and rationalizing turf grass at 6,000 feet in the Great Basin Desert is another matter entirely. Still, I am willing to attempt a modest defense. To begin with, our lawn is quite small, on only one side of the house, and is surrounded by the rest of our property: nearly fifty acres of wild desert that we have deliberately left undisturbed. I never use herbicides on the little yard, the fertilizer I apply is organic and slow-release, and the watering regime is strictly limited and carefully timed for efficiency. Outside the lawn, every tree and shrub I have planted is a local or regional native, most of which are hardy and xeric. The lawn keeps the dust down and has reduced the number of scorpions and rattlers we encounter immediately outside the house. It also works in concert with the wind to act as a giant swamp cooler, helping to make it possible for us to live in the desert without air conditioning—which, in these parts, runs on electricity generated primarily from carbon-polluting coal-fired power plants.

Unlike a suburban yard, our lawn functions as an oasis: the only patch of green anywhere around and the sole moist spot between here and a seep that is 1,000 feet above us and three miles to our west. In an area that receives only seven inches of precipitation each year—and most of that in the form of snow—a little water creates a lot of magic. Modest as it appears, our patch of grass sustains a bumper crop of insects, which, in turn, makes our home not only a haven for Say's phoebes, western kingbirds, mountain bluebirds, scrub and pinyon jays, and many other bug-eating birds but also a refuge for seed eaters like collared doves and California quail. The insects have also made this a terrific place to be a lizard, and we have seen an increase in our populations of both western fence and leopard lizards. And, to my relief, the lawn is cropped so constantly by desert cottontails and big black-tailed jackrabbits that I hardly ever have to mow!

All these insects, songbirds, lizards, and small mammals have, likewise, made the lawn a prime location for raptors and coyotes, which have been quick to take advantage of the food chain reaction triggered by our damp spot. In fact, the coyotes denned so nearby this year that for a month this spring we had the daily pleasure of watching three tiny pups peering out at us from the sage. The lawn has also become an oasis for our girls. I suppose Hannah and Caroline did fine playing in the alkali-encrusted hardpan that existed here before I installed the lawn, but they now seem encouraged to play more games and do more handstands, not to mention enjoy the childhood rite of passage that entails running through a sprinkler after staining your tongue blue with Popsicles.

I admit that this defense of my lawn amounts to morally feeble equivocation, which is why I make sure to keep handy a bourbon barrel–size load of guilt about it. Wallace Stegner wrote that Westerners need to "get over the color green," but my challenge has been to get over having gotten over the color green. Driven to desperate measures by my shame, I recently had the bright idea to rebrand the lawn "the firebreak," which is a concept everyone out here on this wildlands interface understands and respects. This is disingenuous on my part, since I maintain other firebreaks that function perfectly well without being lined with water-dependent, non-native turf grass. But it just sounds better to say "firebreak," so much so that I now insist that we all use that term and that term only, and I fine the girls a quarter each time they slip up and utter "lawn" by mistake. The family is now pretty well retrained, and so it is common for little Caroline to say, "Daddy, I'm going out to do cartwheels on the firebreak."

Henry Thoreau would have seen right through this feeble apologia, and he would have instantly called "horseshit" my cowardly rebranding of the unsustainable indulgence that is my lawn as a "firebreak." But I do have a longer-term plan to mend my ways. When the girls someday go off to college (hopefully one with a brigade of precision lawn mowers to bring some laughter to those boring parades), I will bring in three end dump truck loads of sand and bury the lawn completely, making a nice little island beach up here in the heart of the trackless sagebrush ocean. In the meantime, I have decided to ditch Thoreau and, instead, go with Walt Whitman, who, in *Leaves of Grass* (1855), testified that "a leaf of grass is the journey-work of the stars." *Journey-work of the stars* just has such a lovely, ennobling, poetic ring to it. It may not be quite as lyrical as "firebreak," but for now I will accept any substitute for that unspeakable, four-letter word: L***.

TIME FOR A TREE HOUSE

Actually, Hannah and Caroline never really asked me to build them a tree house. I came up with that idea myself, got them attached to it, and then pretended that my efforts were strictly for their benefit. But their spontaneous enthusiasm provided the necessary cover for me to do what every grown man secretly wants to do: construct an arboreal retreat, far from unpaid bills and truck repairs, uncertainty about the future, and inescapable news of gun violence or environmental catastrophe and the grief these unthinkable losses engender. Never mind a long weekend in the mountains or going to a baseball game. What I really needed was to climb up into a tree house and pull the rope ladder up behind me, leaving my worldly woes behind.

The problem with building a tree house in the Great Basin is that we have so few trees, and even fewer that provide tolerable support for any kind of structure. Because Ranting Hill sits at almost 6,000 feet, we are high enough to have Utah junipers here, but they are tangled, tight, scratchy trees that are uninviting for inhabitation. As a result, the girls and I devised a plan to build a platform house that would stand on stilts amid a dense grove of junipers. Construction began only once I had persuaded the kids that a platform house in the trees does officially count as a real tree house. Because my main goal was to make the thing so tall that it would produce an exhilarating feeling of being in the treetops, I chose for my main structural timbers four sixteen-foot-long 4 × 6 posts, which I balanced carefully on my shoulder, hauled to the juniper grove, and set up in concrete. This would not only produce inspiring height but also allow a design featuring both a lower and upper platform, making the structure resemble the bunk beds of a desert giant. Next came horizontal 2 × 6 supports, then 2 × 4 cross ribbing, and finally the two floors themselves, each consisting of a full 4 × 8 sheet of marine plywood. After adding an upper safety railing and buccaneer-style swinging rope ladder, the retreat was complete: a thirteen-foot-tall, two-story, sixty-four-square-foot platform house nestled into a thick copse of aromatic Utah juniper.

There is no point in pretending that my desire to build a tree house was not driven by nostalgia. It all began with the 1960 Disney film *Swiss Family Robinson*, based on Johann David Wyss's 1812 novel of the same title. As a kid I loved that movie, which fueled the pastoral fantasy that I could not only escape school but even leave the earth, clambering up into a treetop hideaway from which no grown-up could make me descend—not even to wash up for supper. And I was not alone. The popularity of that crappy movie bankrolled the "Swiss Family Treehouse" replicas that sprouted up at Disney parks not only in southern California, but in Paris, Tokyo, and Hong Kong as well. So popular were these reproductions of the movie's elaborate tree house that the Anaheim version lasted from 1962 until 1999, when it was converted into "Tarzan's Treehouse" as a tie-in to the Disney Tarzan film released that year. The big-screen *Swiss Family Robinson* was itself influenced by the immensely profitable *Tarzan* film franchise that began during the early 1930s. In fact, any kind of tree house movie provides a quick way of separating a guy from his money.

The contemporary version of this fantasy is evident in the passion the ultra-rich have developed for tree houses. This opulent fad has gained so much traction that there are now more than thirty luxury tree house design and construction firms in the United States and United Kingdom alone, and many of the tree houses they build are not only nicer, but also larger than the houses most of us live in. Who, you might ask, would be crazy enough to pay six figures for a tree house? The answer is simple: any guy with a ton of scratch who saw *Swiss Family Robinson* when he was eight years old.

This bizarre indulgence has led, inevitably, to Finca Bellavista, an upscale tree house *development*, built high in the jungle canopy of Costa Rica. The Animal Planet network now features a reality TV show called *Treehouse Masters*, in which tree house guru Pete Nelson exposes us to pornographically lavish tree houses while simultaneously pretending that a tree house with running water, air conditioning, stained-glass windows, and a martini bar qualifies as a minimalist sanctuary enabling a Thoreauvian reconnection with nature. But while Nelson's claim is patent horseshit, it is irresistible horseshit of the kind few of us can live a single day without. You might object that tree houses are meant for kids and that the adult longing for one is nothing more than a puerile expression of a desperate desire to escape, momentarily, the pressures of adult responsibility. To which I reply, *exactly*! That is what makes a tree house so cool, even and especially after one grows to adulthood, realizes that *Swiss Family Robinson* is total crap, and then wants to watch it again anyway.

Believe it or not, there is historical precedent for the luxury tree house craze, as some sixteenth-century Italian aristocrats constructed arboreal retreats in their elaborate gardens—you know, just to provide them an escape from the pressures of the main mansion. In other cultures, tree houses have more practical uses. The Korowai, a Papuan people of southeastern Irian Jaya, live in virtually unassailable tree houses at least 100 feet up; this is a precaution they take against their neighbors, the Citak, who are reputed to be headhunters. There is even some argument that a desire to inhabit trees is braided into the double helix that preconditions human behavior. Roughly six million years ago, we hominids parted ways from the evolutionary ancestor we share with chimpanzees and bonobos, but there could still be some deep-time muscle memory at play here. After all, we share more than 95 percent of our DNA with chimps—and nearly the same amount with bonobos, the central African dwarf chimpanzees whose DNA is even closer to human DNA than it is to the DNA of gorillas. To judge by Caroline, the human-chimp genetic convergence appears to be closer to 99.99 percent. Could it be that there is just something in us that wants to climb trees—and, once up there, wants to build a nest, skip school or work, and hang out peeling bananas or shaking martinis?

There is one other cultural context in which tree houses have figured prominently, and that is the amazing tree-sitting protests that have been used to save old-growth forests from logging and also to protest mining, protect Native American property rights, and preserve urban green space. A daring variation on civil rights–era sit-ins, protest tree-sits began in New Zealand during the late 1970s but spread to Australia, Tasmania, Canada, and the United States, where they have occurred in California, Oregon, Washington, and West Virginia (where they were used to protest and delay mountaintop removal coal mining). One urban tree-sit in Berkeley, California, lasted twenty-one months, and even the mainstream media covered the protest of the Humboldt County activist Julia "Butterfly" Hill, who spent a remarkable 738 consecutive days in "Luna," a fifteen-hundred-year-old coast redwood, from 1997 to 1999. Once in the trees, activists not only build tree houses—where they live for weeks, months, or even years—but also connect those houses from tree to tree, creating a webbed network of cables and rappel lines throughout the canopy. One anti-logging protest tree village in central Oregon's Willamette National Forest had more than a thousand activists in the trees at various times, and included such practical amenities as composting toilets, hydroponic sprout farms, and lock-on points for activists to chain themselves to during forced evictions.

In his beautiful 1972 book *Invisible Cities*, Italo Calvino describes Baucis, an imaginary city that exists in the sky, rests upon slender stilts, and is populated by people who never descend to the ground. "There are three hypotheses about the inhabitants of Baucis," writes Calvino. "That they hate the earth; that they respect it so much they avoid all contact; that they love it as it was before they existed and with spyglasses and telescopes aimed downward they never tire of examining it, leaf by leaf, stone by stone, ant by ant, contemplating with fascination their own absence." It strikes me as ironic that our children are so anxious to grow up, because they desire the freedom from authority they imagine adulthood will bring, while at the same time we grown-ups crave a return to childhood in order to evade the burdens adulthood actually entails. I wonder if there will be some magic day on which my beautiful daughters and I will pass each other, they rushing forward in a desire for adult responsibility, I rushing backward through memory and imagination in an attempt to escape it.

Our tree house on Ranting Hill, though modest in comparison to the one depicted in the old Disney film, is well concealed among the juniper and seems perfectly exotic to us. It satisfies our innate craving to retreat to a secret hideaway, one whose stilts lift us into the trees from which we clambered down so long ago. While our tree house is only about 250 feet from home, it remains invisible, secret, always ready to become a pirate galleon, desert island, lunar module, raven's nest, hot-air balloon, or undiscovered planet—whatever we need it to be. Maybe a sanctuary for a too-grown-up writer, engaged in a one-man tree-sit protest against adulthood. Our tree house provides a place to climb above the weary earth for a moment, if only to gaze back down at that earth and contemplate with fascination our own absence from it.

HARVESTING THE DESERT SHOE TREE

O N THE WEST SIDE of our home mountain, whose rocky crest delineates the invisible line separating the Silver and Golden States of Nevada and California, there is a curiosity that has long puzzled and charmed me. Out along a lonely stretch of two-lane not far from Hallelujah Junction, so named because it is the only place in this long valley where we desert rats can load up on the essentials—water, whiskey, and fuel—there stands a strikingly tall and graceful Utah juniper. This unusual tree rises in a grand, angular gesture from a sandy flat of sage and rabbitbrush. Its height, open structure, and twisting musculature distinguish it from the low, bushy junipers up and down the valley, making it a kind of natural monument. Any southbounder rolling in from Mount Shasta country or the Lassen lava lands can feel in the dark just where this tree stands: past Red Rock canyon, beyond the mule deer migration tunnels, not far from the Hallelujah resupply. But what makes this tree special is something stranger: it is festooned with hundreds of pairs of shoes.

I have long wondered why the desert shoe tree possesses such appeal. How did this tree become a celebrated landmark, one we always stop at, even though we can't say why? Why do Hannah and Caroline consider it such a treat to visit the tree? Why don't we see the shoe tree as an abomination, a site of litter at best and of desecration at worst? One possibility is that, excepting the road itself, the desert shoe tree is among the only signs of human culture along this remote stretch of the Fremont Highway. Perhaps the loneliness we feel out on the empty road is diminished by this strange reminder that we are not as alone as this valley's isolation might lead us to believe.

Or maybe it is pure novelty that attracts us to the desert shoe tree. If every tree in the valley were draped with shoes, would we instead pull over to photograph the one tree that lacked them? Sometimes, it seems the tree represents a kind of freedom, an un-burdening that occurs when we not only throw something away but throw it with all our might, flinging some discarded frag-ment of our lives away forever. Or are we compelled by the pure aesthetic beauty of the form: a giant, graceful, organic structure, carved into the desert sky, with hundreds of parti-colored blos-soms dangling and twirling in the incessant sweep of the Washoe Zephyr? Or do we simply crave the thrill of doing something so playful, so unfettered? Wouldn't it be more responsible to keep and wear those shoes a little longer? Absolutely. And that is why we bust a gut trying to sling them into the very highest of this tree's outstretched branches.

Of one thing, however, I am absolutely certain. These shoes tell stories. Some do so literally, because their hurlers have in-scribed them with a dizzying variety of names, dates, messages, and odd pearls of wisdom. Our daughters notice that "Jenny" has explained, on the bottom of her flip-flops, that she is on her way home to Portland from a transformative week in Yosemite. "William" has shed an expensive pair of wingtips, leaving a note on the sole to tell us that he has just married "Maria" up in Feather River country. The recent date on a low-hanging baby shoe celebrates the birth of "Cezar," while a pair of deck shoes, whose rubber sole is inscribed "For Great Grandma," may commemorate a passage in the other direction. And here we discover a pair of dangling army boots that are fully annotated with their story. They were worn in a faraway war zone by "Ansaldo," who is, at last, home safely to the western Great Basin, and who reminds passersby that "Freedom Is Not Free." Welcome home, Ansaldo, wherever and whoever you are.

The less-storied shoes provoke us to craft narratives that remain unwritten, as we are drawn into making them meaningful by their type, condition, and placement. Could those dangling cleats indicate that an ace closer pulled over to toss them in a victory celebration, or do the castoff spikes mark the unfortunate conclusion of a career ended by injury? Do those high heels mean that a newlywed passed by on her way to a new life, or did she discard them to celebrate retirement from a cubicle she waited thirty years to escape? Do the work boots symbolize a flight from a lifetime of hard labor, or does the weight of their steel-toed construction simply make them satisfying to launch?

The girls and I take turns pointing out different shoes and guessing the stories of their wearers and slingers. We make a great deal more of the shoes' narratives than the scant evidence will support, but that may be why we love the desert shoe tree so much. It is a strange field for the imagination—one in which we discern our own feelings, memories, and hopes. Each time we return to the tree it bears new fruit, and we pause not only to collect but also to invent its stories.

Last Sunday, our family made a pilgrimage to the desert shoe tree for two very important reasons. Hannah had outgrown her sparkly, high-top Chucks, and it was time to keep my promise that she could attempt to bola-whip them into the arms of the celebrated tree. The second and more important reason involved Caroline, who is the kind of kid for whom a parent plans not college savings but rather bail money. Several years ago, Caroline had resolved to root for the LA Dodgers, which she did solely to perturb the rest of the family, since we are, like all sensible northern Great Basinians, devoted fans of the San Francisco Giants. Although I found this mindless act of rebellion troubling, I rationalized that Caroline would soon return from the dark side—that she would outgrow this foolishness, just as Hannah had outgrown her sneakers.

As the season wore on, however, I was reminded that Caroline's rebelliousness is matched only by her stubbornness: she is part cute little girl and part cross-eyed mule. First, she saved her meager allowance money, bought a Dodgers cap, and refused to take it off, even in bed. When she adopted Dodger blue as her wardrobe color of choice and continued to cheer loudly for the Giants' arch rivals deep into the following season, I explained, as clearly and patiently as a loving father can, what it means to be "disowned." She remained unfazed, carrying her poor behavior into a third season, at which point I felt obliged to describe, in rich, imaginative detail, the terrible "kiddie prison" awaiting her if she failed to change her ways. She replied that there are probably TVs in kiddie prison, which would be convenient, because she could "chillax and watch the Dodgers kick some Giant butt."

After three years I at last relented and told the kid she could be a Dodgers fan so long as she legally changed her last name. And that was the magic moment in which little Caroline, having bested me, resolved to become a Giants fan. My act of reverse psychology was as effective as it was accidental, and suddenly she had joined the family in rooting for the correct team.

"Mom and I are so relieved!" I exclaimed. "What can we do to celebrate this great day in our family?"

Apparently, Caroline had already thought this through. "Take me to the shoe tree," she replied without hesitation, "and I'll climb it and leave this stinky Dodgers hat up there with all those stinky shoes."

We had a nice visit to the shoe tree that day. We saw some pronghorn gliding across the open desert, heard a few croaking ravens, caught the pungent smell that crests from the shimmering, wind-driven waves of this vast sagebrush ocean. First up was Hannah, who, after repeated attempts, discovered that it is quite challenging to whip a pair of shoes high into the air. It requires just the right backswing, timing, and follow-through. She soon got the hang of it, though, and managed to lodge her sparkly Chucks at a respectable height.

Next came the main event. Little Caroline wrote her initials on the brim of her Dodgers cap, and Hannah added "GO GIANTS!!!" for good measure. Then Caroline—who by now was wearing the Giants ball cap we had given her—climbed up into the shoe tree and, smiling widely, hung her Dodgers cap on a branch of the juniper. "I'm the first one who ever put a hat in the shoe tree," she said. "And since nobody ever did that before, it's a hat tree now, and I thought that up." I wonder if that is how the first person to toss their shoes into this tree also felt.

If you are ever driving at dusk down a lonely two-lane in the western Great Basin Desert, out on the Nevada-California line, past the red canyon above Hallelujah, and you see carved into the sky a giant tree full of hats, my kid thought that up. If there is still a Dodgers cap in it, you will know just what it means to harvest the sweet, blue fruit of its small story. It means that the people who unburden themselves here have found a way to leave their past behind.

MOST LIKELY TO SECEDE

I T IS LESS THAN NINETY MILES, as the raven flies, from Ranting Hill to Rough and Ready, California, a town in the western
Sierra Nevada foothills that holds special meaning for a reclusive
curmudgeon like me. Rough and Ready was settled as a miners'
outpost in 1849, after which it quickly grew to be a boomtown of
three thousand. Just a year or so after its settlement, though, the
people of Rough and Ready decided they were already fed up with
the constraints of citizenship, and so they held a gathering at which
they voted to withdraw from the Territory of California and secede
from the United States. On April 7, 1850, the Great Republic of
Rough and Ready was established, and for several months it made
out just fine as one of the tiniest and most independent nations in
the world.

On July 4 of that same year, or so the story goes, the men
of Rough and Ready ran into trouble when they rode the four
miles to nearby Grass Valley to get good and drunk. (During the
mid-nineteenth century, Americans were both more patriotic and

more inebriated than we are today—so much so that even temperance societies had little choice but to offer their members a reprieve from the sobriety pledge on Independence Day.) But, to their dismay, the thirsty men of Rough and Ready reached the Grass Valley saloon only to be told that they were now considered "foreigners" and thus would be served no hooch—especially not on the day set aside to celebrate the great nation from which they had chosen to secede. Sticking to the principles most important to true patriots, the men quickly convened another meeting, voted resoundingly to rejoin the United States immediately, and then returned to the Grass Valley saloon, where cheers went up as the newly reassimilated Americans set patriotically to get hammered on corn liquor along with their fellow countrymen.

The tale of the Great Republic of Rough and Ready has a curious addendum. Just after World War II, the US Postal Service discovered that Rough and Ready had never formally been readmitted to the Union and so had, essentially, been operating as a rogue nation for nearly a century. A few forms were filled out, and on June 16, 1948, Rough and Ready formally rejoined the United States. No doubt there was more heavy drinking to celebrate the occasion. These days Rough and Ready has a population of about nine hundred folks, approximately seven hundred of whom would shoot you just for stepping onto their porch; the other two hundred are telecommuting San Francisco Bay Area software designers, which is far worse. But I do love to think of the long century during which Rough and Ready existed both within and outside the nation that did and did not quite contain it.

There is a long tradition of secessionist movements in America, a country itself formed through breakaway. Though we often associate secession with the Southern states that confederated against the Union during the Civil War, folks all over the country have been talking about getting out ever since they got in. Texas was once a free country (it seceded from Mexico rather than the United States), eight counties of western North Carolina existed briefly as the State of Franklin, Maine was born when it seceded from Massachusetts, and both Kentucky and West Virginia were formed through secession from Virginia. There have been a slew of fifty-first state proposals, from folks in Michigan's Upper Peninsula aspiring to become a state modestly named "Superior" to Long Islanders whose inherent sense of superiority motivated them to try to avoid slumming with the rest of New York. Northern California began trying to declare itself free of southern California even before the establishment of Rough and Ready and, in fact, has never stopped trying. A number of entire states—the usual suspects, including Vermont, Alaska, Hawaii, Texas, and California—have attempted to remove themselves from the country. The citizens of countless cities and counties have also followed Rough and Ready in attempting to sever themselves from the United States. Following the outcome of all recent presidential elections, secession petitions have been filed from nearly every state in the nation.

Perhaps most interesting are regionalist and bioregionalist secession movements, which have been strongest in the West. In 1849, the same year Rough and Ready was founded, the Mormon church established the independent state of Deseret, which occupied most of the Great Basin. Communities around Yreka, California, have tried to leave the Union to form the State of Jefferson, an ongoing effort since 1941, when some independent-minded folks declared they would attempt to secede from the United States "every Thursday until further notice." In the Pacific Northwest, advocates are attempting to form the bioregional state of Cascadia, which would comprise parts of a number of US states and even British Columbia. Some Lakota people in Wyoming, Montana, Nebraska, and the Dakotas have created the Republic of Lakota to emphasize that they never chose to join the nation in the first place.

Crazy as they might sound, attempts to live within a larger political structure while somehow escaping its constraints make a kind of sense. Conceptually, secession speaks to our urge to declare ourselves independent from systems we find inefficient, unjust, or constraining, though we tend to look right past the privileges and utility of social confederation. We are all for decent roads and also against the taxes necessary to maintain them. I think it is human nature to form compacts and then rebel against their power over us. The urge to withdraw from most everything is intense out here in Silver Hills, where those of us who survive the fires, earthquakes, aridity, wind, snow, and rattlers have implicitly declared a fairly extreme form of independence simply by choosing to dwell here.

Secession means not only "formal withdrawal from an organization" but also "withdrawal into privacy or solitude." In this latter sense, I am a secessionist of the first order. In fact, I wonder if I should follow the inspiration of my neighbors in nearby Rough and Ready and formally declare the absolute independence of our place here in Silver Hills. I already feel myself to be more a citizen of the western Great Basin than of Washoe County, and I am more a desert rat than a Nevadan. What if I could succeed in seceding from this county and state and instead establish the 49.1-acre Great Republic of Ranting Hill?

Some things would change straightaway. No one who roots for the Dodgers is allowed into the kingdom. The tribute required when entering the Republic of Ranting Hill is a box of IPA, payable down at our green farm gate. This, by the way, is the full extent of my immigration policy. No light beer is permitted to cross the border without imposition of a steep import tariff: a pint of porter is owed for every three light beers transported (unless they are also misspelled "lite," in which case the tariff escalates to two pints). People who whine on hikes or arrive late for fishing trips do not receive a return invitation. Anyone abiding in the Republic will be required, at some point during their residency, to own a donkey that wears a straw hat. People who describe the desert using the pejoratives "empty" or "barren" automatically receive an official declaration of imbecility, while those who support the disposal of nuclear waste in the Great Basin will face extradition to Idaho. I have also declared an immediate end to sentimental pining for greenness, and anyone who can't tell you their elevation and name a half dozen desert wildflowers or birds will be required to perform community service in the form of weed-whacking. Drunken plinkers and illegal off-roaders are barred from the kingdom but will be subjected to witty heckling from across the frontage border fence—which has a high-strung, barbless bottom strand, to allow pronghorn to pass in peace. I have also declared a moratorium on the discussion of trivialities such as religion, politics, and economics, but that's just common sense.

My most significant act as the benevolent dictator of the Great Republic of Ranting Hill has been to appoint Hannah and Caroline to my cabinet, a leadership move made after observing that children tend to be more sensible than adults. So now the Rules of the Republic also include no bullying, cutting in line on the monkey bars, or making fun of your sister's glasses. Bed making is now optional in the Republic, and, until further notice, healthy breakfasts have been replaced by an endless supply of Froot Loops. Mom will serve as vice president and is charged with attending the state funerals of goldfish. All employees of the Republic have, as part of their compensation package, sparkly shoes and one free Popsicle per day. The official motto of the kingdom is "Girls Rule, Boys Drool," though my cabinet will need to reconcile this with the fact that our national anthem is a song by a boy band—though at least the band has a fitting name: One Republic.

Ultimately, what matters most about the Great Republic of

Ranting Hill is not the specific rules that govern our citizenry but the spirit of absolute independence in which we operate. This radical autonomy is pure fantasy, since even the road that takes us from Silver Hills to town is kept up by the state of Nevada and leads to a highway maintained by the feds. But out here in the Great Republic, which is defined only by big wind, scorching heat, and alpenglow on distant peaks, the concepts of state and nation seem mere abstractions. Maybe there is a way to split the difference: we will declare our absolute independence but also celebrate July 4. I hereby decree that everybody gets booze. Even foreigners.

PLANTING THE DOG

THE OTHER DAY, while rummaging through a stack of un-sorted papers, I came across a card that was mailed to me about this time last year. Noting by the return address that it was sent by our veterinarian, I surmised that it would be a standard-issue expression of regret for the loss of our old dog, Darcy, who we had paid good money to have the vet put down a few days before the card arrived. Reasoning that I might as well have a look before tossing it into the recycling bin, I opened and read the card. It contained a stock expression of sympathy for "Darcy" (unneces-sary quotation marks get quite a "workout" in American "English"). "You made a caring decision," read the message, which was nestled in a field of delicate little paw prints.

Well, OK, I thought. This is more sympathy than most folks get when they lose an uncle, and although the card misused quotation marks and did not contain a discount coupon, the sentiment was compassionate. But included within the card was a smaller card containing the text of a poem that I had seen on display in the special room within the vet's office where customers must wait with their soon-to-be-euthanized companions. A truly atrocious poem of uncertain provenance, "Rainbow Bridge" is six stanzas of mawkish reassurance not only that our dead dog will go to heaven but also that we will be reunited with her there. This struck me as an ambitious claim, especially compared to "you made a caring decision," which seemed reassuring without presuming too much about the afterlife.

According to "Rainbow Bridge," dead dogs end up in a grassy meadow that functions as a timeless purgatory between heaven and earth, where they hang out in a roving pack of fellow mutts, until that magical day when they cross over said bridge into an interspecies heaven where they experience a blissful moment of reunion with their human pal. A single stanza of this literary gem will suffice:

> For just at that instant, their eyes have met;
> Together again, both person and pet.
> So they run to each other, these friends from long past,
> The time of their parting is over at last.

Even setting aside the deplorable quality of this ditty, which made me wonder if I should ask the vet to administer the pentobarbital to me instead of to Darcy, there are a number of problems here. First, the poem presumes not only that readers are onboard with the concept of heaven, but also that they want a pack of dogs around when they get there. The poem does not specify whether there are fleas, ticks, or canine flatulence in heaven or whether, in the suburban parts of heaven, you are expected to pick up your angel dog's feces with a plastic bag.

Even if you do subscribe to the idea of heaven, and even if you do not mind a bunch of yelping dogs joining you there, consider some other problems with the "Rainbow Bridge" account of immortality. If this is really heaven, how do we know that all pet owners will make it through the pearly gates? Judging by my Silver Hillbilly neighbors, I would be surprised if half of us are admitted into the land of fish fries and harp recitals. We are more likely to end up in a place as hot as the desert—but one with more whiskey, which we might prefer in any case. And what of the dogs themselves? Assuming that the canine Saint Peter (or is it Saint Bernard?) has any standards at all, you need to figure that most of these shoe-eating, garden-destroying butt-sniffers are more likely to be reunited with their masters in the underworld.

I am also appalled that this poem is so patently illogical. Why relegate dogs to the timeless verdant meadows first? How about just sticking the nonheaven end of the rainbow bridge into the vet's office and expediting the process of doggie salvation? Then there is the troubling point that, while this card is intended to reassure me, it presupposes that I am consoled by the contemplation of my own mortality. Sure, I would like to be with Darcy again, but when it comes to reuniting with the dead, whether human or canine, my goal is to put it off as long as possible. Finally, the card from my vet indicates imprecisely that this poem is "inspired by a Norse legend." This is an indirect reference to the Bifröst Bridge, which, in Norse mythology, is a burning rainbow that links this world, called Midgard, to Asgard, the realm of the gods. But the thirteenth-century Icelandic *Eddas* clearly foretell the collapse of this bridge, which, in any case, is perpetually aflame and spans a river of boiling water—an apocalyptic vision of the afterlife that is a far cry from the blithe reassurances of the insipid "Rainbow Bridge."

But here is the problem with making fun of this crappy poem: it hurts like hell to lose your dog. As I waited with Darcy for the vet to come into the room to dispatch her, I was as choked up as

I have ever been. Researchers who study emotional attachment and separation have found that the bonds we have with our pets are often comparable to those we have with fellow humans. To make matters worse, we are often confused about how to reckon the loss of a pet, because in the case of these nonhuman loved ones, our culture has no accepted ritual of parting—unless you are willing to count reading "Rainbow Bridge" through streaming tears in a veterinarian's office. The nerds who study this stuff have coined the term "disenfranchised grief" to refer to a form of very real sadness that we nevertheless are not quite sure we are allowed to feel. As one grief geek observed, "socially sanctioned mourning procedures, such as funerals, do not occur following the death of a pet, even though research shows that it is critical to the healing process."

We named Darcy for the song "Darcy Farrow," which features references to western Nevada's Walker River and Carson Valley, and includes these words in its final stanza: "They sing of Darcy Farrow where the Truckee runs through, / They sing of her beauty in Virginia City too." She was a wonderful dog, a true member of our family who was affectionate and gentle with our young daughters but also tireless in the field with me. I have done the redneck math: Darcy and I walked more than 10,000 miles together through these remote desert canyons, playas, and mountains. It is impossible to share that much time with a dog—that many memorable experiences of this astonishing land—and not become bonded in a deeply meaningful way. Several years ago, Darcy was pack hunted by a band of coyotes and was sliced to ribbons before making a narrow escape. When she came limping home, her fur matted and blood-soaked, I thought she was a goner. But the vet shaved her down and stitched her up, and though she looked like a canine Frankenstein for several months, she recovered fully and lived to walk another few thousand miles with me.

When it came time to say good-bye, it did no damned good to tell myself that Darcy is "just a dog." As a confirmed desert rat, I knew that I should take my dog, gun, and shovel out into the sage and take care of this myself. But when that inevitable day arrived, I could not do it, and that is how I became a reader of "Rainbow Bridge." That is also how I came into possession of a small cedar box containing the ashes of a dog, which were produced at additional expense when, in an already excruciating moment, I learned that Darcy's body would be disposed of as "clinical waste." What difference should it make what becomes of a dead dog, however much beloved in life? I still do not know the answer to this question, but in that moment it was an easy call to trade money for the assurance that my 10,000-mile trail companion would not leave this world in a dumpster.

The morning after my visit to the vet, sleepy-eyed little Caroline said, "Dad, I had the most awesomest dream last night. I dreamed that right before they burned Darcy, her heart started beating, and she came back and lived with us, and I was able to pet her, and her fur was so soft. And then I woke up, and it was all a dream, and I'm really sad now."

Summer is coming to an end. The unusual desert rainstorm that has blasted us for two days has ended, and the sky is clearing now. The wildfire up in the hills to the south has finally been extinguished, and the Washoe Zephyr has at last ceased howling. I am taking the little cedar box, a wooden-handled shovel, and an ice-cold IPA, and I am hiking up onto a nearby hillside that is graced by a pair of old junipers. Between them, I will dig a small hole in this sandy soil before raising a toast to Darcy and our shared trail. Then I will kneel down among the sage and plant my dog.

As a final gesture, I will stand at attention and read aloud the terribly sappy "Rainbow Bridge." Although it will be impossible for me not to laugh, it is also certain that I will weep, because both

are so necessary. If ceremonies of mourning are essential to grieving, and if our culture lacks rituals of parting from nonhuman
friends, then we will just have to act like the resourceful, imaginative people we are and invent one of our own. My newly developed ritual will be inadequate, but it is a memorial gesture that
must pass for reunion here in this remote western desert, which is
our only earth and also our only heaven.

MY HOME LAKE

EDWARD ABBEY began *Desert Solitaire* with these words: "This is the most beautiful place on earth. There are many such places." My home lake here in Silver Hills is the most gorgeous place on the planet, in just the way Cactus Ed intended. It is nestled in a gently sloping basin surrounded by granitic hills that are dotted with bitterbrush and big sage. In the spring, balsamroot and lupine cover the upland slopes in a drapery of bright yellow and purple, while the pink flush of desert peach ignites the rocky draws. In autumn, golden domes of rabbitbrush appear everywhere. Green fingers of ephedra, which emerge from a blanket of snow in winter, are grazed by pronghorn and mule deer. My home lake is also a jewel on the necklace of the Pacific inland flyway, and is home to at least eighty species of birds. All year round we see golden eagles here, and harriers, red tails, kestrels, and ravens, great horned owls, western kingbirds, mountain bluebirds, and horned larks. So perfectly lovely is this place that when it came time to marry, I decided to hike Eryn to the top of the nearby hills. There, on a crisp fall day just like this one, we rested on granite boulders, gazed out across the stunning expanse of the lake, and decided to spend our lives together. In this place, as in no other, there is a stark clarity of light, a rippling play of shadow, a catharsis of wind that makes you want to begin your life anew. There is one more thing I should mention about my home lake: it contains no water.

I realize that some people are so shamefully effete that they might expect a lake to have water. Some folks may even think they *deserve* to have water in a lake—they are spoiled enough to feel entitled to it. It would not surprise me if there are even people who would argue that a big, empty basin of land without a drop of water in it should not be called a lake. I suspect these are the same folks who drive across the desert without so much as slowing down and report back that there's "nothing" there. Well, that same nothing fills my home lake, and those of us who live here do not see our lake as being empty of water. We see it as being full of light and wind. Full of coyotes and rattlers. Full of the kind of space that only the high desert can hold—space that is crowded out of other landscapes by irritating obstructions, like trees and water. Even if there are no trees blocking your view, how can you really see a lake if the damned thing is all filled up with water?

Although my home lake is what is called a *dry lake* or *alkali flat*, such lakes exist around the globe and are graced with a variety of lyrical names: *kavir* in Iran, *takyr* in central Asia, *abkha* in much of the Arabic world, *pan* in South Africa, and *salar* in most of South America. The term most widely used in Mexico and in the Intermountain West is *playa lake*. To scientists, this is an *endorheic* lake, which is a hydrowonky way of saying that it exists in a closed basin in which water flows in but never flows out. Moisture arriving here by any means will either evaporate or be absorbed into the ground. In this kind of internal drainage system, the concept of "downstream" simply does not apply. This special place is where water comes to die, and to be reborn.

An endorheic lake such as this one has a dry bed—around here we call the lakebed a *playa* (Spanish for "beach")—which is among the flattest landscapes on Earth. This is why desert playas are used for rocketry and for setting land speed records. It is also why huge playas like Smoke Creek and Black Rock are the site of Nevada's signature form of outdoor recreation. First, drive your truck out onto the playa. Then, weight the accelerator pedal with a chunk of granite or jimmy it with a bitterbrush branch. As the vehicle begins covering ground, tune the radio to the baseball game, then clamber out your window and onto the top of your truck's cab. Be sure to take the six-pack with you. Now, sit back and enjoy the sun, the breeze, and the scenery of the distant mountains as your unmanned truck drives itself randomly across the expansive sublimity of one of the most isotropic landscapes on the planet. Wear your shades, because playas are bright white from a coating of fine-grained saline sediment that contains evaporative minerals such as borax and sodium carbonate. The playa is also the cradle of fantastic dust storms, as rising spirals of hot desert wind whip the white dust into towering gyres that can be seen for many miles. Recent research even suggests that the particles liberated from playas in this way act as condensation nuclei: they are the seeds from which clouds are grown in the wild garden of the sky.

My grandpa, who, I am proud to say, was a home brewer during Prohibition, used to tell me stories of accidentally oversugaring beer batches and having the bottles explode beneath the beds where they were hidden. "A lot of people wet their beds back then," he used to joke, "from the bottom up. Pop! Pop! Pop!" Playa lakes are often created in the same way: they are flooded from below. Even in the absence of runoff from snowmelt, it sometimes happens that the water table beneath the playa rises high enough to intersect the surface, at which point water percolates up onto the endorheic lakebed from below. When that happens, what looks like the sun-baked, rock-hard surface of the playa is actually a thin crust, beneath which looms a subterranean megalake. Every now and then, some uninitiated visitor tearing across the playa at high speed fails to notice the telltale dimples that subtly reveal the upward movement of underground water. No matter. They figure it out when the crust of the playa cracks, like thin ice, and their vehicle is swallowed by the water below.

Like many larger endorheic terminus lakes, my little home lake does have water in it now and then. Even in dry years there is enough subsurface moisture around its margin to sustain tules—the reeds traditionally used by our Paiute neighbors to fashion everything from delicate duck decoys to functional boats to thatching for their sturdy wickiups. Coyote willow, which also grows around the lake, is handy on hard hikes: break off a branch and gnaw it a little as you walk, and its natural salicin, which is chemically related to aspirin, has a mild analgesic effect. If we have had a big snow year, the runoff onto the playa during the melt-out will create a broad expanse of gleaming water, though the lake may be no more than a few inches deep. In those years, it becomes an oasis for wading birds, including stilts, avocets, and ibis of both the white and white-faced varieties. If we have had several wet winters in a row, the lake becomes more expansive and a bit deeper, and, in those years, migrating tundra swans will join the resident Canada geese in wintering with us. In one unusually wet year, we had more than a hundred graceful swans on the lake from Thanksgiving until we uncorked the Redbreast Irish whiskey on St. Paddy's Day. That was the winter we almost forgot that water is not a permanent feature of this landscape. Here in the desert, even a lake is like a swan, an antelope, a wildfire, a moment of clarity. It comes and goes.

In most parts of most years, my home lake is bone-dry, and sometimes it remains parched for so long that it becomes a vast, lovely garden of weeds. It has been perfectly waterless for three years now—just as it was on that shimmering day, sixteen years ago, when I looked out over this light-filled basin and asked Eryn to set aside her usual good sense and marry me. On such a day, who needs water? Besides, I am so accustomed to hiking through the lake that I am not sure I would want to go around it.

A lake without water speaks more to memory and to hope than it does to the kind of certainty that is so rare on this side of the vale of tears. Most of what we love is ultimately transient, and it takes a desiccated resilience to reconcile with that fact. So the term I like best to describe the intermittent, uncertain nature of this endorheic Great Basin playa lake is *ephemeral*. If the ephemerality of my home lake makes it less picturesque, its periodic waterlessness also gives it a hard, bright certainty that inspires appreciation for what it means to live in this world. The water will return in time. Until it does, we will gaze out across this shimmering lakebed and slake our thirst with light.

CHICKENFEATHERS STRIKES WATER

F OR CENTURIES, people have been "dowsing," an activity that is also known by a variety of vernacular terms such as "witching," "divining," and, Hannah and Caroline's favorite, "doodlebugging." Dowsing is the activity of attempting to locate—without the use of scientific equipment—something valuable that lies beneath the ground. In earlier centuries dowsers primarily sought lodes of precious metals, while in more recent times dowsing has more often been used to witch wells—that is, to locate sources of subterranean water in advance of drilling a domestic water well. The devices used by dowsers vary, but most employ some form of "witching stick," which, during the Renaissance, was known as the *virgula divina* (Latin for "divine rod"). This divining rod is often a Y-shaped stick cut from witch hazel, willow, or peach, but it may be made of any number of other materials. In order to appreciate dowsing, you must understand only two things: the practice has been widespread for more than five hundred years; and, there is absolutely no scientific evidence of its effectiveness.

Out here in Silver Hills, our wells are deep, expensive, and sometimes unreliable, and so your good or bad luck with a well often determines not only the value of your property but also its inhabitability. The hit-or-miss nature of drilling for high desert water has given rise to a rich body of local folk narratives, which sometimes focus on the quality of a well as an indicator of human character. For example, we all know the story about our neighbor who went 700 feet, came up dry, picked a new spot, and then went 900 feet before finally discovering sulfurous, fetid, barely potable liquid that leaks out at three gallons per minute. And we all know *why* this guy had to pay north of fifty grand for a dribble of putrid water: because he sided with a local developer who wants to turn some of our pronghorn calving grounds and mule deer winter range into a labyrinth of cul-de-sacs. Meanwhile, the nicest guy on our road went only 300 feet and scored forty-five gallons per minute of liquid gold—a sure sign that he has received his reward on earth, even if it turns out there is no water in heaven. While no Silver Hillbilly would ever mention God, let alone karma, out here in Silver Hills we seem to believe that water, like faith, must be the evidence of things unseen.

Before we could build our passive-solar home, we first had to succeed in sinking a well, so we asked around among Silver Hillbillies about good drillers. The consensus seemed to be that it wasn't who drilled your well that mattered but where they drilled it. And that, rumor had it, was the exclusive province of Chickenfeathers, an eighty-odd-year-old neighbor who was locally renowned as a dowser. While no one on my road would admit to having had the old man witch their own well, each neighbor told me that everyone else on the road had used him to witch theirs.

When I expressed polite skepticism about Chickenfeathers to Ludde, my closest neighbor and my mentor as a curmudgeon, he replied, "You're gonna spend a shitload of dollars on a well no scientist can tell you where to drill. Maybe Chickenfeathers knows where to drill, maybe he doesn't, but he only charges forty bucks. You think you know better?" This from a man who once watched me put my truck into four-wheel drive *after* I was stuck in the mud and asked, "Do you also wipe your ass after you pull your pants up?"

I called Chickenfeathers. He said he was too old to drive, so we made arrangements for my dad to give him a lift out to Ranting Hill. Chickenfeathers turned out to be closer to 180 than eighty, and he was dressed like the Great Basin cowboy he was: roper boots, dusty jeans, plaid shirt, leather vest, silver bolo tie, rabbit-felt cowboy hat with feathers on the face of the crown, and a cow-hide satchel that he wore slung over one shoulder. When he got to our place, Chickenfeathers just wanted to sit on the tailgate and talk and watch the mountains etch the sky. He had lived a long time, and he was a man who was done hurrying.

After a half hour, Chickenfeathers finally opened the leather satchel, from which he removed a curved, forked stick that he said was freshly cut from coyote willow; along with the witching stick he had a smaller leather bag, which swung from a handsome lan-yard artfully braided from thin strips of sagebrush bark. He positioned the forks of the willow rod in his weathered hands, glanced at my dad and me, and said, with total confidence, "Let's find you boys some water."

Chickenfeathers began to wander around the desert in the general vicinity of where we imagined the house might someday be built, zigzagging through the desert peach and bitterbrush like a slow-motion hound working to catch a scent. My dad and I followed along behind him, alternating glances between the witching stick and the old man's face, which wore a look of unrelenting concentration. Chickenfeathers's unhurried approach gave me plenty of time to think about what I was actually doing: paying forty bills for the privilege of watching a cowboy wizard shuffle around in the dust to get his entirely unscientific opinion about where I should bet a lot of money I could not afford to lose. I was embarrassed for engaging in what was clearly pure superstition. What next? Would I pay somebody to find water in the lines of my palm—in tea leaves or a tarot deck? My pretensions to intelligence faded as I admitted that I had now entered the Magic Eight Ball school of problem solving—though I rationalized that my fate may have been sealed when, as a kid, my own Magic Eight Ball cracked, lost its fluid, and remained stuck on "Reply hazy, try again."

"Right here, boys!" called Chickenfeathers, indicating a perfectly random spot in the open desert. "*Right here*," he repeated with confidence. He opened the small leather pouch and took out a silver plumb bob, which was attached to a long string adorned with chicken feathers. He began to swing the feathered bob back and forth hypnotically over the sand, apparently feeling for the water through some invisible vibration along that feathered string, listening for the life-giving water percolating in its rock sanctuary far below the desiccated surface of the Great Basin. "You'll go 400 feet and get twenty-six gallons a minute," he declared, "and that water will be sweet as honey in the rock."

After forking over a pair of Andy Jacksons and then delivering Chickenfeathers to his small house out on a remote BLM inholding, my dad and I tried once again to figure out where to drill the well. We agreed that Chickenfeathers's performance had not inspired much confidence, but we lacked any clear way to make a sensible, informed decision about where to locate the well. The problem seemed to be not where we should drill but on what grounds we could rationalize choosing a spot other than the one Chickenfeathers had recommended with such conviction. In the absence of hard facts, it seemed natural to have recourse to

39065153362429

Betteridge, Susan Jane

Pickup By: September 22, 2018

pure superstition, and so, eventually, we simply gave up and drilled where Chickenfeathers said we should.

When the drilling was done, we had gone 440 feet and struck almost thirty gallons per minute of water that is more delicious than words will ever tell. I have no way of knowing if Chickenfeathers was correct, or just lucky. I know only that I got my forty bucks worth no matter what is true, no matter what remains hidden. We do not know where those invisible, subterranean rivers flow, or how to find them, or what it means even if we do. But there is an old kind of listening that reminds us of the sweet water that is always down there, somewhere.

ANECDOTE OF THE JEEP

NINETEEN nineteen was a decent year for America, all in all. The Grand Canyon received protection as a national park, the Nineteenth Amendment at last gave women the vote, the world witnessed the end of the war that was to have ended all wars, and American heroes Jackie Robinson and J. D. Salinger were born. Then again, 1919 was not all good. The Volstead Act initiated Prohibition. There were the infamous Palmer raids against political and labor "agitators," many of whom were deported for the obscure crime of "undermining American society." It was also the year of the Great Molasses Flood, in which two million gallons of viscous, saccharine goo from a ruptured distillery tank flowed in a fifteen-foot flash flood down the paved slot canyons of Boston. And the American poet Wallace Stevens had the bright idea to put a jar in a wild forest in Tennessee. "Anecdote of the Jar," his 1919 poem documenting this bizarre experiment, begins this way:

> I placed a jar in Tennessee,
> And round it was, upon a hill.

It made the slovenly wilderness
Surround that hill.
The wilderness rose up to it,
And sprawled around, no longer wild.

I am no expert on poetry, but this little gem has always struck me as horseshit. Anyone who has been to Tennessee will testify that folks there do not leave empty a jar that might be handy for holding shell casings, poker winnings, dentures, or moonshine. And I doubt we need a poet to reveal the profundity that a jar is round—especially not a poet so lazy that he would rhyme "hill" with "hill." Most troubling, though, is Stevens's haughty denigration of wilderness. *Slovenly?* I'll hazard a guess that the wilderness is at least as well ordered as the closet of your average poet. And does Stevens actually believe that his little jar can make the wilderness rise up and relinquish its wildness? We get a lot more truth from Wallace Stegner than from Wallace Stevens. After all, Wallace of the West wrote not only that "something will have gone out of us as a people if we ever let the remaining wilderness be destroyed," but also "I despise that locution 'having sex,' which describes something a good deal more mechanical than making love and a good deal less fun than fucking." With that kind of insight and literary expressiveness, can it be any surprise that Stegner won the Pulitzer Prize? While Stevens deserves some credit for having once punched Ernest Hemingway in the face, it should be noted that the blow broke Stevens's hand, after which Papa proceeded to administer a humiliating drubbing.

But I must confess that my certainty about Wallace of the East's misunderstanding of wilderness and wildness has been challenged by my recent discovery of an unusual piece of trash in a remote desert canyon out here in Silver Hills. A few weeks ago, as I was hiking some knobs and draws about four miles northwest of Ranting Hill, I emerged from a rocky traverse and suddenly spotted the wreck of a Jeep in the canyon bottom below me. It was a captivating sight, and rather than being appalled that this lovely spot had been littered with a wasted car, I was instead fascinated by it. First of all, the Jeep was no beater but was a late-model, bright red Cherokee. This is significant, because we do not drive red cars in rural Nevada, where we live by the tacit but inviolable rule that "look at me" colors should be confined to places like suburban Connecticut, where Wallace Stevens lived. Then, there was the fact that the Jeep had been blown to smithereens by everything from .22 pistol rounds and peppered shotgun blasts to the heavier damage inflicted by high-powered rifle fire. In one sense, the Jeep was still a Jeep, but in another sense it had simply become a large, red, perforated object that, like Stevens's empty jar, resided awkwardly in a place where it did not belong.

There was also an appealing sense in which the Jeep had become naturalized. Its cherry red paint had already begun to fade in the unrelenting sun, and the winds channeling through the throat of the canyon had coated its seats and floorboards with a thick layer of alkali dust. Giant, white poopsplosions on the crumpled hood showed where a raptor had used the Jeep as a hunting perch, while the interior of the vehicle had already been repurposed as a pack-rat nest—one not only woven from sage branches and studded with owl pellets but also consisting of taillight shards, tufts of carpeted floor mats, foam from shredded bucket seats, and fragments of shattered mirrors that glinted from deep within the stick nest. Jackrabbit tracks surrounded the ruin, and bone-studded, taper-tipped coyote scat was also nearby.

Then, there was the mystery of how the Jeep came to rest in this inaccessible place. It could have tumbled from the cliff above, where an obscure two-track marks the route to an old prospect hole that was hand-dug by pocket hunters who hoped the silver in Silver Hills was not played out, but the Cherokee showed no structural damage consistent with rolling. Or it could have been wrecked before it arrived here, maybe dropped by one of the CH-47 Chinook helicopters that sometimes use this remote desert for training exercises. Both explanations seemed unlikely. And while it would be extremely difficult to *drive* a vehicle to this spot, it did at least seem possible. If that is what actually happened, this could have been the work of rebellious teenagers, who nabbed the car in Reno and took a joyride that resulted in more of an adventure than they bargained for. Or, the car may have been hotwired and used in the commission of a crime, after which the crooks needed to make it disappear.

Or, maybe the road trip that ended here was taken by some desperate man—a poet, perhaps—who went out one evening to buy a loaf of bread, began to think too much about his past, and just kept following these remote desert two-tracks until he ran aground in this sandy wash bottom and could sail no farther. Maybe he climbed out of his Cherokee, stood for a moment with the door wide open and the radio playing, took a deep breath of the sage-filled night air, and then simply left the keys to all the doors in his life swinging in the ignition. Perhaps, while walking across the open desert by starlight he was transformed, and at daybreak he reached a gravel road, flagged down a hay truck, climbed aboard, and vanished into an entirely new future.

The Jeep is not a jar, but its presence in this isolated desert canyon raises some of the same questions posed by Wallace of the East's empty vessel. To inquire into the story of the wreck is to ask for its meaning, which is a question I prefer not to ask out here—a question I never ask of granite or sage. As Stevens's poem seems to predict, though, the Cherokee has become a landmark in my imaginative cartography, a location I frequently visualize and seem magnetically attracted to. Now, when I set out to visit the spring or collect blue quartz or track pronghorn or search for owls' nests, I often find that the arc of my walk is deflected toward the wreck. The wilderness of the desert does seem to rise up and surround the blasted Jeep, much as Wallace of the East claimed that the wilderness of a Tennessee forest once encircled his jar. Stevens is right that the presence of this cultural artifact has altered my relationship to nature in this place. But I believe he is wrong to suppose that any jar or Jeep can deprive this land of its wildness, for if the Jeep has been deserted, in the sense of "left behind," it is also becoming *desert-ed*—made a part of this spectacular arid landscape, into which it is already beginning to vanish. Here is no antiseptic placement of a hollow jar but, rather, a stunning site of wreck and abandonment—one infested by rodents and bleaching to pink bones in the sun. In some sense that I do not yet understand, this perforated chunk of industrial waste confirms my sense that wilderness, which not only surrounds the Jeep but swallows it utterly, remains undomesticated here. While the wreck adds a dot to the imaginative map of my home territory, it also reaffirms that this is a vast, unforgiving, wild country in which our absolute freedom and our eventual abandonment remain equally certain.

MOCKINGBIRD
ON THE WING

WE NATURE WRITERS do a lot of windy sermonizing about
the value of staying put. We celebrate the decision to strike
roots, encouraging readers to inhabit their home landscape with a
commitment and passion that will allow them to resist the transience that has characterized American culture since the first prairie schooner set sail for the sunset. And it is clear enough that in the
West this frontier mentality has resulted in the sorts of problems
you'd expect from folks who see their place as a temporary stop on
the way to some imagined better place just beyond the next ridge or
range. I myself have staged a quiet rebellion against transience, digging in and making my stand out here in the remote Great Basin.
In fact, once the Amazon drones start delivering whiskey to these
arid hinterlands, I may never go to town again.

The problem with this bioregional evangelizing can be summarized with a single word: *October*. When the wind picks up
an autumnal chill and the nights turn cold, when the clock falls
back an hour and the stove wood needs hauling before the snow

flies, when the World Series comes to an end and the long winter looms, I experience an irresistible restlessness. In the opening lines of his wonderful poem "How to Like It," Stephen Dobyns captures perfectly the feeling I experience each October:

These are the first days of fall. The wind
at evening smells of roads still to be traveled,
while the sound of leaves blowing across the lawns
is like an unsettled feeling in the blood,
the desire to get in a car and just keep driving.

In praising rootedness, we environmental writers have chosen our central metaphor from the plant world. But what if we derived our core concept from fauna rather than flora? We might then adopt a metaphor of movement or migration rather than rootedness, for everywhere around us we see animals passing through. October in the high desert is the time when mule deer and pronghorn move downslope to avoid blizzards and mountain lions. Critters of every stripe are in high gear, driven by the shortening days to cache the supplies necessary to survive encroaching winter, while seasonal birds are stopping by on their way to warmer climes. Perhaps the most natural thing for me to do in October is not hunker down and strike roots but instead make contact with my animal self, get on the move, and light out for some unknown territory.

A rare visitor who has recently joined us on Ranting Hill has me thinking about these issues of rootedness and transience. Although the northern mockingbird is so widely distributed as to be a regular neighbor to many Westerners, in more than a decade out here we had never before seen one. The first appearance of this remarkable guest occurred several weeks ago, when out of nowhere an unmistakable flash of white-barred wings appeared in the sagebrush. The bird has remained with us since then, and I wonder if it has come to make a home in this remote desert outpost or, as is more likely, is passing through on its way to a more hospitable place. For now, we are enjoying the bird in the same way we enjoy the final days of fall, with no certainty about how long the pleasure might last, and with a haunting feeling that it will soon be shut from our view as the doors of winter swing closed.

Unlike other desert birds, most of which are fairly retiring, our Ranting Hill mockingbird is gregarious, loquacious, almost fearless. It struts around on its tall, skinny legs, proudly holding its long tail up high behind it, acting like it owns the place. It perches on the lawn furniture and appears bothered when we head outside to check on the weather. It snags insects on the bare ground and in the low scrub but also visits our woods rose and silver buffaloberry bushes to diversify its diet with native, autumnal fruits.

The main thing Ranting Hill mocker does is sing. First described by Linnaeus in 1758, the mockingbird's modern scientific name is *Mimus polyglottos*, which means "many-tongued mimic." It is a name the mockingbird richly deserves, as individual birds routinely have thirty or more songs, and in some cases even up to two hundred! While these many melodies most often mimic the songs of other birds, the mockingbird's repertoire also includes mimicry of the sounds of insects, frogs and toads, and even mechanical noises. I first became aware of our visitor when I heard a bird song that was unfamiliar to me. Before I could solve the mystery of this new song I discerned a second tune I'd never heard before, and then a third. If only one new bird had appeared, many new songs had arrived with it, as if a flock of exotics had come to our home, like a visiting circus. Our mockingbird is a one-bird band, an avian karaoke machine, a multilingual messenger who hails from distant lands, carrying with it all their varied music. I've even tried to communicate with the bird by playing it blues riffs on the harmonica. While it hasn't yet consented to jam with me, it does seem interested, and I have not yet given up trying.

Because mockingbirds are now so common and so widely dispersed, many of us are unaware of how rare they once were. During the late eighteenth and the nineteenth centuries, a flourishing caged-bird trade decimated populations of many songbirds in America, including the cardinal, indigo bunting, and that most impressive of singers, the mockingbird. A 1904 issue of *Bird-Lore*, a publication of the Audubon Society, celebrated the passage of new legislation protecting nongame birds, while also reminding readers of what was at stake: "A few weeks since the [Audubon Society] Chairman visited the store of a bird dealer in New York, and in one large cage saw not less than sixty Mockingbirds, some of them so young that when the cage was approached the poor birds hopped to the wire netting fluttering their wings and opening their mouths to be fed."

The most famous American to keep a mockingbird as a pet was Thomas Jefferson. In November 1772, Jefferson purchased his first mockingbird from a slave for five shillings. At that time the wild mockingbirds that now grace the woods surrounding Monticello were still decades away from expanding their range to Virginia, and so the species was a true novelty. Jefferson would go on to own at least four mockingbirds, several of which were able to mimic the woodland birds of Virginia and also sing American and Scottish songs. In 1784 Jefferson even took a mockingbird with him to France and back, a trip during which the bird learned not only to sing French songs but also to imitate the creaking of the timbers on the ship that carried it across the broad Atlantic. Jefferson also has the distinction of being the first US President to keep a pet in the White House. His companion mockingbird, Dick, not only lived in the presidential mansion but in fact had free range within it. Jefferson routinely left Dick's cage open so he could fly around, perch on the president's shoulder while he worked, even sing duets with Jefferson as he played the violin. Jefferson's appreciation for this unique species is apparent in his suggestion to a friend that he should teach his children to honor the mockingbird as "a superior being in the form of a bird."

Jefferson's idea that the mockingbird is "a superior being in the form of a bird" is also present in many Native American cultures. The Cherokee embraced mockingbirds as the embodiment of cleverness and intelligence, while Hopi and other Pueblo peoples told stories in which the bird was the bringer of language who taught the people to speak. Further west, Maricopa Indians believed that dreaming of a mockingbird was a sign that the dreamer would soon receive special powers. Shasta Indian culture considered the bird a sacred guardian of the dead, while Papago and Pima folklore figured the mockingbird as a mediator whose song functions as a bridge between the human and animal worlds.

The most prominent reference to the bird in Anglo culture appears in the late Harper Lee's 1960 classic, *To Kill a Mockingbird*, a book much beloved by our daughters, as well as by their mom and dad. In the novel, Atticus Finch tells his kids that "it's a sin to kill a mockingbird." When Scout, the young girl who is the novel's narrator, asks her neighbor, Miss Maudie, for clarification, this is the reply she receives: "Mockingbirds don't do one thing but make music for us to enjoy. They don't eat up people's gardens, don't nest in corncribs, they don't do one thing but sing their hearts out for us. That's why it's a sin to kill a mockingbird."

I like to think of the Ranting Hill mockingbird as being in a kind of temporary artist's residency, the way a visiting writer, painter, or musician might be. This bird has come from elsewhere to warble its unfamiliar tunes, and perhaps also to gather things: insects, berries, western meadowlark song, this bittersweet, late-season, low-angle shaft of high desert sunlight. I suspect that this remarkable bird, whose appearance here is unprecedented and unaccountable, will soon be moving on. A messenger between seasons and between worlds, the mockingbird is a transient whose existence is rooted in the air, a fleeting gift of autumn that makes its stand on wings.

WHAT'S DRIER THAN DAVID SEDARIS?

LIKE ME, David Sedaris is a literary humorist. Unlike me, he has sold around eight million copies of his books, which have been translated into twenty-five languages and counting. (Several of my essays have been translated into Estonian; I may not be big in Japan, but the Estonians find me hilarious.) As any insanely jealous fellow writer would, I have been busy finding *reasons* (which Eryn unkindly refers to as *excuses*) why Sedaris has been a bit more successful than I have. Why do I reckon Sedaris is outselling me? Well, though raised in North Carolina, he writes from an estate in England, while I write from a remote hilltop in a sparsely inhabited western desert. His neighbors are intelligent, cultured, literate people with beaucoup leisure time and disposable income. My neighbors are less interested in a good laugh than you might think. This is because my neighbors are scorpions, rattlers, and libertarian survivalists—the latter of which can be dangerous.

An actual incident involving David Sedaris visiting my town bolsters this theory while also supporting my corollary assumption that Sedaris, who must certainly be fearful of competition from me, is out to discredit those of us here in the Intermountain West. It all started after Sedaris did a reading in Reno while on a sixty-city book tour. Soon after his stop here in northern Nevada, Sedaris appeared on the satirical television news program *The Daily Show*, where host Jon Stewart inquired about the many cities he was visiting. "Which one did you hate the most?" quipped the host. Sedaris replied with a story about his observations at a recent reading in Reno. The humorist observed, wryly, that "the icebreaking question when I was signing books was, 'Why did you choose *that* T-shirt?'" He went on to criticize the Nevadans' attire, which he claimed included sweatpants and cut-off shorts. The punch line of the anecdote concerned a woman in her sixties who approached Sedaris to have her book signed. "Is that your *good* Count Chocula T-shirt?" Sedaris asked the woman. "I didn't think anyone was going to notice," she replied. The anecdote was masterfully calculated and timed, and Sedaris had Stewart and his New York City audience in stitches. So that's the story. It made the usual cyber-rounds and was soon enjoyed by folks across the nation.

I generally subscribe to the ageless principle that there is no such thing as bad publicity, but the Sedaris-in-Nevada incident went largely without scrutiny, and so I feel the need to examine it more closely. First, let me say that I do not blame Sedaris for stooping so low to get a cheap laugh, since this is something I do at every possible opportunity. Second, I have no interest in defending the informal dress of Nevadans, because it strains my imagination to think of anything less interesting or important. Finally, I certainly will not spill any ink speculating about the veracity of Sedaris's anecdote, because, as a humorist myself, I know very well that whether any of this actually occurred is immaterial.

No, my objections are different than you might suspect. First, I believe a person should know what the hell he or she is talking about when making fun of something. As a single example, consider this gem from the late Robin Williams: "Do you think God gets stoned once in a while? Look at the platypus. I think so." If you know, as Williams clearly did, that the duck-billed platypus is an egg-laying mammal—that is to say, a total oddball in the animal kingdom—then this joke will be funny to you, even if you aren't stoned. Sedaris, by contrast, clearly doesn't know Reno from his other fifty-nine whistle stops. Exhibit A: in chatting with Stewart, he doesn't even pronounce the name of our state correctly (it's NevAda, not NevAHda).

Equally egregious, the comic who offers this excoriation of how we dress has chosen, for his national television appearance, thick horned-rim glasses that make him look uncannily like that cartoon dog Mr. Peabody, a shirt in a bright pink reminiscent of cheap cotton candy, a tie the color of dung, and, as the pièce de résistance, black dress shoes worn with white socks. Seriously? Sweatpants would have been a clear improvement on this get-up. Apparently, though, the outfit is to Jon Stewart's taste. "You look terrific," he tells the humorist. "Very nice suit." Sure, so long as it's Halloween, and you're costumed as a pseudo-intellectual Woody Allen. Stewart's acumen is on further display when Sedaris describes folks at the event wearing cut-offs. "Was it a particularly hot and humid environment?" asks Stewart, without a whiff of irony. I went to college with Jon, and he is the smartest funny person (or funniest smart person) I have ever met. That said, *humid in Nevada?* He was never that daft around our freshman dorm.

Even if I could get past the idea that a comic, of all people, would be so pompous as to imagine there should be a dress code at his gigs, I am still deeply insulted on behalf of the truly innocent victim in this story: Count Chocula. In this Halloween season, it seems only right that I should stand up for this slandered hero. General Mills debuted Count Chocula, Franken-Berry, and

Boo-Berry (the "Monster Cereals") back in 1971, which put me at just the right age to love them, and to join the ranks of kids who experienced a condition actually called "Franken-Berry Stool," in which the heavy red dyes in the strawberry-flavored cereal turned our feces the color of David Sedaris's shirt, when they would, under normal circumstances, have been the color of his tie.

Nineteen seventy-one was none too placid a year. The Charles Manson murder trial was nightly news, Ku Klux Klansmen were arrested for bombing school buses, Lt. William Calley was found guilty of the My Lai massacre in Vietnam, and the Nixon administration arrested thirteen thousand antiwar protestors during a single three-day period. Closer to home, Operation Grommet proceeded apace, as the United States spent the year continuing a decades-long program of attacking Nevada (which they probably pronounced NevAHda) with nuclear weapons. It was a moment in which some unnameable innocence was being lost, which is another way of saying that we *needed* Count Chocula. TV commercials even reassured our parents that the cereal was "so full of nutrients, it's scary!" Not as scary as the A-bomb, or even the fuchsia poop induced by Franken-Berry, but you get the point.

As for the count himself, he could hardly have been *less* frightening. He was, in fact, a sweet little vampire, with his single fang (like a kid who has lost one of his front baby teeth), huge doe eyes, comically pointy ears, long puppet nose, and friendly, silly grin. (Actually, I detect a slight resemblance to Sedaris.) One of the unique personality traits of the cartoon vampire was that, although he had the power to scare the other cereal monsters in his posse, he was often terrified when he came face to face with children. Yes, you heard that right. We children, in an age of fear, had the power to scare a vampire! It was a delicious feeling, knowing that we could turn the tables on terror simply by lifting our spoons.

Now that I am a father, the proposition that children are more terrifying than vampires seems obvious enough. Each fall, when the monster cereals are sold for a short time leading up to Halloween, I become unapologetically nostalgic. That the cereals have been successfully rereleased in special edition retro boxes suggests I am not alone in this. Count Chocula? Come on, Sedaris. He's one of the good guys.

So here is a summary of how the notorious incident with David Sedaris and the Reno T-shirt lady appeared to the national audience of *The Daily Show*: Sedaris hilariously satirizes Nevadans' attire, building to a punch line in which the sixty-something T-shirt lady is comically exposed as ignorant and provincial. Indeed, she is figured as doubly stupid, first for wearing the shirt, and then for failing to realize the humorist's joke is at her expense.

Here, instead, is how I characterize the incident: While dressed like a cross between an editor at *The New Yorker* and a boozed-up birthday party clown, a comic who is raking large coin in our community mispronounces the name of our state on national TV while failing to answer the host's inane query as to whether it is unusually humid in the high desert. Finding it amusing to insult an older woman who has paid handsomely to see his show, purchased his book, and waited in line to meet him, he delivers a sarcastic crack about a T-shirt bearing the image of sweet old Count Chocula, whom anyone who was a kid in 1971 would now support for president.

As a humorist myself—which is to say, as a person for whom irreverence must be understood as my stock-in-trade—I do not have a problem with *any* of that. But here is what chaps my hide: Sedaris fails to realize that it is not he but instead the Reno woman who delivers the punch line, of which Sedaris himself is the butt. "I didn't think anyone was going to notice," she replies, without missing a beat. The irony in this exchange belongs not to the humorist for observing the idiosyncrasy of the woman's informal attire but rather to the woman, who knows perfectly well what Sedaris is doing and bests him by turning the joke around with the kind of graceful, self-deprecating irony that is the hallmark of genuine wit. (And can there be any doubt that she is a person of good humor if she has chosen to wear her Chocula colors to a performing arts center?) Every desert rat knows that this brand of dry humor is a signature characteristic of those of us who dwell in this dry place.

Sedaris is right that this is an amusing anecdote. He is simply wrong about *why*. So I hope one of you reading this will let him know that black socks go with black shoes and teach him how to pronounce *Nevada*. (You might also mention to Jon that Nevada is the driest state in the Union.) Most important, please tell David Sedaris—whom I consider the most gifted literary humorist working today—that it is *we* who consider *him* the unwitting provincial. You think *The New Yorker* has cornered the market on irony? Out here in the desert West, our irony is so damned dry that it's scary. *Bluh! Bluh! Bwaa haah haah!*

HUNTING FOR SCORPIONS

WHILE HANNAH IS THE family intellectual, Caroline is a tireless athlete, which is why Eryn and I were surprised when Caroline chose "Ancient Egypt" for her day-camp class. For five days she immersed herself in the culture of an ancient people who, like her, were intrepid desert dwellers. On the afternoon of her third day in camp, Caroline brought home her freshly made drawing of an Egyptian goddess.

"What is that cornucopia-looking thing on top of this lady's noggin?" I asked Caroline.

"Come on, Dad. Can't you tell? That's a big ol' scorpion!" she replied with genuine enthusiasm.

"No kidding? Weird place for a scorpion. What's her name?"

"It gets spelled different sometimes, but basically it is S-E-R-K-E-T. Six or seven thousand years ago, she was supposably the goddess of stings and bites. A lot of the old Egyptian people thought she could protect them from scorpion stings. There was even a gold statue of her in there with King Tut!" she explained. "Pretty epic, huh?"

I may have been in detention in the principal's office during the ancient Egypt unit in my own educational past, but somehow the scorpion on the head thing struck me as improbable, and seven thousand sounded like too many years, even for so ancient a culture. But a little research convinced me that Caroline had her story straight and that Serqet (or Serket or Selket) was indeed a powerful goddess dating back to the predynastic period of Egyptian culture, which flourished between about 5500 and 3100 BCE.

As a deification of the scorpion, Serqet represented genuine power in a culture for whom lethal scorpion stings would have been a very real threat. Her full name, "Serket hetyt," contains an intriguing dual reference to the gruesome asphyxiation that can be caused by a bad sting. The name may mean "she who tightens the throat," a clear allusion to the toxic power of the scorpion and its representative goddess, or "she who causes the throat to breathe," which instead suggests her power to protect or restore those who might otherwise perish from a sting. The scorpion is common in ancient Egyptian art. Among the earliest hieroglyphic signs was the scorpion ideogram, which is found written in papyrus texts, carved into ivory and wood, and chiseled into stone monuments.

The evolutionary biologist J. B. S. Haldane once observed that the Creator must have "an inordinate fondness for beetles," because beetle species are so impressively numerous. He might well have added that the Creator seems to like scorpions pretty well too. More than seventeen hundred species are known, and they exist on every continent except Antarctica. The fossil record is also rich in scorpions, and we know that this fascinating animal has existed in some form for around 450 million years, making it one of the oldest terrestrial invertebrates on the planet. There are scorpions in caves, in jungles, on prairies and savannahs, even high in the Andes and Himalayas. As the goddess Serqet reminds us, however, scorpions are most abundant in deserts. Of the ninety or so species in the United States, almost all are found west of the Mississippi River, and most live in the arid and semiarid regions of the West. Here in Nevada we have around twenty species, and while some of those exist only down in Mojave country, up here in the Great Basin we have scorpions aplenty. They range from tiny little guys all the way up to the Northern Desert Hairy Scorpion (*Hadrurus spadix*), which can be almost six inches long—large enough to eat mice, lizards, and other scorpions.

We humans specialize in being afraid of things (and people, and ideas) we do not understand. While this spontaneous fear may retain some modest adaptive value, often it causes us to act like small-minded dummies and, even worse, to miss out on a lot of things that are remarkably cool. Many people would include scorpions, along with their cousins the spiders (both are arachnids and neither is an insect), in the category of "the only thing I know about this animal is that I am scared of it." It is true that all scorpions sting and all are venomous. And, yes, they like to hide in places where they are difficult to detect and then ambush their prey—or your foot—in a vicious attack. And, sure, they brutally crush their victim in their pinchers while stinging it with a paralyzing blast of neurotoxins and enzyme inhibitors before subjecting it to a tissue-dissolving acid spray, after which they coolly slurp it up. But is this treatment any worse than what we rural Westerners are subjected to by our local county commissioners? Young children (other than county commissioners) are at greater risk. The Mayo Clinic reports that after receiving a sting, little kids may experience convulsions, drooling, sweating, and inconsolable crying. If this is an accurate description of symptoms, I hereby submit that all five-year-olds everywhere are being stung by scorpions all the time. I will allow that anyone who is allergic to scorpion venom is likely to have a rough time of it, but why malign these little arthropods when the same might be said of a damned peanut?

Not many scorpions in the United States have a very potent sting. Southern Nevadans have to worry about the notoriously toxic bark scorpion, which likes to crawl up walls, hide behind framed pictures, and then creep out at night to drink your best whiskey before attacking and devouring you as you sleep. But I doubt even this fate could crack the top-ten list called "Risks of Visiting Vegas." Here in the northern desert, our scorpions all have friendly little stings that are somewhere between a harvester ant's bite and a honey bee's sting. And since we have almost no gnats, chiggers, ticks, fleas, mosquitoes, horseflies, wasps, yellow jackets, or hornets, we need something that can sting just to keep us from getting too soft.

One of the many amazing things about scorpions is that they glow in the dark. To be more specific, they glow under ultraviolet light. There has been considerable debate about why a scorpion should have this in common with the 1970s fuzzy poster of a ghost ship on the wall of your parents' basement that ignites under what stoners used to call "black light." Some have maintained that this glow trick is a random accident of evolution, which is a theory that strikes me as both unlikely and just plain lazy. Others have wondered if the fluorescence is used to help scorpions hunt, but there is no solid evidence to support this theory. Nor does it seem likely that the glow warns predators or allows communication between scorpions, though both explanations have intuitive appeal and do remain possible.

The current and most likely explanation for scorpion luminescence is far more incredible. Start with the fact that although scorpions have one pair of eyes atop their cephalothorax ("head-chest") and another two to five pairs along the front sides of their cephalothorax, they have crummy eyesight. To be more precise, they have decent sight within the blue-green spectrum and truly lousy vision outside it. Now, add to this that the main hazard of being a scorpion is that it might be spotted by moonlight (they're nocturnal, after all) and get picked off by a predatory lizard, snake, rodent, or bird. The best way to avoid this fate is, obviously, to take cover. But how can the poor scorpion know whether it is being illuminated if its (many) eyes are unable to detect the wavelength of light that emanates from the moon?

It appears that their elegant solution has been to evolve a cuticle that is charged with beta-carboline and other luminescent chemicals. When the scorpion's exoskeleton is struck by moonlight—which, as a reflection of sunlight, contains some of the same UV rays you use sunscreen to protect yourself from—it glows. In this sense, the scorpion's entire body functions as an eye, one that is highly sensitive to very small amounts of UV light. If a scorpion sees itself luminescing—which it can only because the wavelength of that luminesce falls in the blue-green spectrum—it knows that it is exposed and must seek cover. Somewhere deep in its 450-million-year-old nogginchest, the scorpion says to itself, "Dang, my ass is glowing again. Better head for the sagebrush!"

Last night, my buddy Steve—who, along with his wife, Cheryll, has the distinction of having been stung by a scorpion—rolled up to Ranting Hill to lead me on a land lobster expedition. It is essential that one have the proper high-tech equipment before undertaking this challenging and dangerous adventure. Please listen to me carefully, dear reader, because your life could depend upon being properly outfitted. You must have *all* of the following gear: a UV flashlight (ten bucks at the hardware store) and whiskey. To go afield lacking either could be risky.

Steve and I set out just after dusk, knowing we had only ninety minutes before the rising of the full moon, which would flood the desert with light and send scorpions into hiding. (Remember the glowing butt epiphany?) It was also a breezy night, which is not ideal for a scorpion search. Because the animal stalks insects by detecting vibrations through sensory organs in the tips of its legs and specialized hairs on its pincers, wind can disturb its hunting strategy. Despite all this, it took only a minute or two for scorpions to pop out in the purple beams of our flashlights. Steve found one at the base of a native shrub I had planted just a few days before, while another was down by my woodpile, and a third near the girls' tree house. As we headed into the open desert, we discovered others near juniper snags, around sage and bitterbrush, in the rice grass, and even on sandy flats between patches of balsamroot, whose dry leaves rattled gently in the breeze. Some of the scorpions held motionless, like tiny lobsters. Others crawled along slowly. Yet others scurried with surprising speed to avoid us and tuck into their burrows, which are marked by small, arched holes in the desert floor. The scorpions glowed beautifully beneath otherworldly splashes of bright purple as our UV beams tunneled through the darkness.

When I looked up from one of our finds to survey the moonless sky, I noticed reddish Mars and bright, blue-white Spica unusually close to each other in the West. Hanging low in the south was Scorpio, the giant, gracefully curved constellation known since the time of the Babylonians as a scorpion. The unmistakable reddish gem of Antares (which means "rival of Mars") shone brightly from the center of its celestial cephalothorax.

I am only slightly ashamed to admit that the high point of the evening was ogling scorpion sex. Steve called me over to witness two scorpions doing what arachnophiles call the *promenade à deux*, which is a classy, Frenchified, nonpornographic term for the unique mating "dance" of the scorpion—an elaborate process that can take many hours and is highly ritualized. First, the male grasps the female's pedipalps (little mouth claws, like those seen in spiders) in his. Then, he dances her around looking for a good place to deposit his spermatophore, the sperm packet that she will hopefully take into her genital operculum, thus triggering release of the sperm.

This courtship dance can also involve "juddering," in which the scorpions shudder and convulse, and the "cheliceral kiss," during which the male uses his pincers to hold the female's pincers in a gesture that looks, to my human eyes, like holding hands. When this ritual dance is complete, the male retreats quickly, probably to avoid being gobbled up by his partner. Scorpions are ovoviviparous, which means that the young are hatched within the female and only afterward born into the world. Once outside the female, the tiny scorplings will crawl onto her back and hang on there, until they have molted once and are ready to light out on their own.

I have neighbors who say that in their many years of living out here in Silver Hills, they have never seen a scorpion. In ninety minutes of night hiking, Steve and I discovered eighty scorpions, two of which were dancing for the future, and each of which is an amazing, glowing little packet of 450 million years of evolutionary brilliance. I find it fascinating that in all this wide, wild, windy desert, nothing glows under UV light save the scorpion. What if we had a flashlight that emitted a beam that illuminated only spiders and another that ignited only snakes and another that revealed only rodents—or, better yet, separate wavelengths for antelope ground squirrels, kangaroo rats, and bushy-tailed packrats? What if we were capable of matching the astounding diversity and richness of life in this sagebrush steppe biome with a mode of perception that was equally revelatory?

After thinking deeply about our ability—and, more often, our inability—to perceive nature, Henry Thoreau observed, "The question is not what you look at—but how you look and whether you see." To say that the Great Basin is barren is to admit an inattentiveness that is the perceptual equivalent of blindness. Those who dismiss this landscape as empty may be looking at it, but they are not seeing it. This desert is emitting its spectacular beauty in a wavelength that their eyes are not yet evolved to detect.

BEAUREGARD PUPPY

FOR SOME TIME NOW, Hannah and Caroline have been hard at work trying to convince me that grieving for Darcy was over, and we needed to get a new puppy on Ranting Hill. At last I have ceased resistance. In the past I have always owned mongrel bitches that I fetched from the pound for a few bucks and a pledge to spay. But this time Eryn suggested that I should not impose my own lack of good breeding on the new family pet, and so she instead proposed that we complete an online survey to determine which breed of dog would be right for us. It is now clear I should never have agreed to this human-canine compatibility quiz, but at the time it seemed harmless enough to tap a few keys and build a profile of the perfect dog. Did I want a pooch that would be tireless in the field, better behaved than my children, not lap up toilet water like our worthless cat, and stay mellow even when I wail on the blues harp? You bet! So we clicked a bunch of boxes and out popped the result: English setter.

I had never heard of an English setter, and, frankly, I didn't like how . . . well, how *English* it sounded. Since my agency in the family has long been reduced to weed-whacking and drinking whiskey (not always in that order), it was soon decided that we would fork over a mountain of cash to score this dog from a breeder on the California side of the Sierra. I am too embarrassed to confess how much this puppy cost, but it was exactly the same amount I would have paid for a Stihl MS 291 chainsaw with a twenty-inch bar, which is something I have long wanted. The upside was that after securing puppy-naming rights, I insisted on "Beauregard," which I taught the girls to pronounce with a ponderous, jowly Southern drawl. Caroline was quick to perfect her "Southern accident," as she innocently called it, and soon was a dead ringer for the rebel rooster Foghorn Leghorn after a few too many mint juleps.

The day the eleven-week-old puppy arrived on Ranting Hill, I experienced a Nevada-size case of buyer's remorse. "He's *sooo* cute!" the girls squealed as Eryn rehearsed his pedigree in a futile attempt to reassure me.

"His father, Uncle Raleigh, was a great bird dog, and Kaycee, his mother, was an award-winning show dog," she said. The fact that Beau's father was his uncle seemed not only confusing but also potentially incestuous, while the dad's name, Uncle Raleigh, just sounded painfully *English*.

Even more troubling was Mom's name. "Uncle Raleigh and *Kaycee?*" I confirmed. "So Beauregard is the product of one of those royal scandals where the rich aristocrat fathers a bastard child with a prostitute?"

Try as I might, I did not see in Beau the kind of good-looking dog that a sensible guy would swap a decent chainsaw for. He had a skinny little body, but with an oversize head that looked like the wrinkle-faced head of a very old man, which gave him a creepy look. His legs were thin as willow sticks, but at their ends were lynx-like paws about the size of catcher's mitts, suggesting that if he grew into those feet he would weigh as much as a ten-point muley buck. His tail was the classic, bird-dog pointer tail, only it had a sharply angled crink where it looked like someone had slammed it in their tailgate. His skin was absurdly loose and baggy, which—along with his droopy, red eyes—made him look like a wino wearing a speckled, thrift-store suit three sizes too large. His ears were so long that they dragged along in the dirt whenever he walked, and each time he lowered his muzzle to the water bowl those dangling ears would go submarine, surprise him, and he'd come up with a startled headshake that strafed water all the way up the surrounding walls.

Worst of all, this puppy had lips so preposterously long and flappy that he looked like an animal evolved to evade predators by rolling itself up in its own baggy face. Never have I seen such a bizarre sight as little Beau, with those crazy lips the size of a pelican's pouch, sitting patiently while the hot desert wind, catching between his cheeks and gums, flapped his giant lips up and down in a fluttering rhythm that sounded like a baseball card slapping in the spokes of a revolving bicycle wheel—though, to make this analogy accurate, the bike would also have to be covered in dangling strings of viscous slobber. It could not have been an accident that Beauregard was actually born on April Fool's Day.

Beau's behavior was even worse than his appearance. First of all, he did not walk like a dog at all but, rather, like a drunk cowboy, tottering as he moved forward and sideways at the same time. He was also uncoordinated, with none of the grace and precision you would expect in a respectable bird dog. Every time he lifted his rear leg to scratch his head he would miscalculate and miss his noggin completely, causing him to fall over—after which he would look up with a dopey, surprised expression, as he racked his pea brain to reckon what might have gone wrong.

Beau also had a wagonload of rude habits. The abundant lip flaps on his crumpled face were perfectly adapted to amplify his already thunderous snoring, which continued unabated during the twenty hours a day he remained snoozing. In fact, his snoring sounded very much like the chainsaw I was by then so anxious to trade him for. During his few waking hours, Beau would eat about thirty pounds of antelope scat, which was the culinary delicacy he preferred whenever he wasn't chewing on rocks. This unusual diet not only resulted in an endless trail of pronghorn poop, which dropped one pellet at a time from the hidden caverns of his prodigious lips, but also produced flatulence so toxic that I banished him to the garage, where I then feared that the pilot light on the propane hot water heater might ignite a methane explosion. And while I had bought this dog, in part, to have a pet that would scare away critters, it turned out that Beau was terrified of jackrabbits, cottontails, and even ground squirrels. He did, however, love to attack the toy monkey the girls bought for him, so if western Nevada is ever overrun by tiny squeaking chimpanzees, I'll be all set.

Within a week, I had generated a variety of nicknames for Beauregard. When he was especially dim-witted, I called him "SLOWregard." When he snuffled harvester ants out of his nostrils, I referred to him as "BLOWregard." I told him often that I held him in "LOWregard," though that was only because when I gave him commands, he responded with absolutely "NOregard." I was eventually persuaded by Eryn that it was in poor taste to call him "BeauRETARD," though I failed to see how a house pet that routinely wolfs down antelope feces was much in need of respectful treatment.

After a few weeks, though, I decided to cut little Beau some slack. After all, he had come to Nevada from Northern California, where his greatest threat was having chardonnay dribbled onto him by the breeder lady, whose face was partially paralyzed by Botox—which should, instead, have been administered to this wrinkle-faced puppy (BEAUtox?). But now this poor guy was in the Great Basin, where he was being hammered by wind and blasted in the high desert furnace, not to mention getting regular snootfuls of danger in the form of ravenous coyotes or the several species of birds big and fierce enough to pluck his baggy little ass off Ranting Hill, never mind the bobcats and mountain lions. His very first week out here Beau had a run-in with an eleven-button rattler in the garage, which is the kind of thing that can get stuck between your ears—especially if they are as huge as Beau's are. In fairness to the pedigree puppy, Silver Hills is the kind of primitive, exposed country where even human newcomers suffer from a vague fear that they might be carried off by a pterodactyl.

Beau's only good habit is that he wakes me up every morning at around 4:00 A.M. to go outside and pee, which means that I go outside and pee with him. I whiz first, after which slow Beau gets the hint and takes a turn, for which I praise him decisively: "FLOWregard, well done, boy." Taking a leak exhausts him, so he flops down with his giant lip flaps parked in the dirt on either side of his broad snout. This is my cue to sit on a nearby boulder and take in the arched dome of the sky.

On this chilly night the wind has settled a little, and I can just make out the high-pitched yips from an upcanyon band of coyotes. The signature scent of sagebrush sweeps across the open desert. Soaring through the forking light bridge of the Milky Way is the unmistakable asterism of Cygnus, the swan, whose brightest star, Deneb, is blazing at its tail as it cranes its long, graceful neck toward the mountains. At last, the spiral light of Venus crests the desert hills to the east.

Reconsidering sleepy Beauregard by starlight, it now seems that he might fit right in here. After all, we not only tolerate eccentricity in Silver Hills, we all but require it. If Beau is weird looking, poorly behaved, ill-mannered, comical, and glaringly imperfect, then he has all that in common with me—and, perhaps, with every desert rat who has chosen to make a life in this hard, wild place.

DESERT INSOMNIA

E VEN AFTER ALL THESE YEARS, I do not recall precisely
what I was thinking when I decided it would be a good idea to
move out to this isolated desert hilltop. Surely, it must have had something to do with a desire for solitude. No less an authority on pastoral
bliss than Billy Wordsworth wrote that, "with an eye made quiet by
the power of harmony, and the deep power of joy, we see into the life
of things," and so I had been persuaded that true insight must be correlated with harmonious silence. If I could get away from the relentless
din of humanity—so little of which has substantial or lasting value—I,
too, might gain the power to see into the beauty of this Great Basin
landscape and the strange and amazing life we live within it.

In conflict with this fantasy of silence is the fact that I am a
father, for there is no refuge from the incessant torrent of noise
that we parents both produce and are subjected to. Trying to parent
and have quiet is like trying to swim without getting wet. It is not
only the girls' talking that breaks the silence around here; it is also
their regrettable habit of waking throughout the night and feel-

ing obliged to come tell me all about it. The other night, Caroline marched into our bedroom at 1:45 A.M. and blurted out, "Do you think, if you crossed a camel with a monkey, it could go without water and still climb trees?"

I replied as any exhausted parent would. "Do you need to know the answer tonight, honey, or can I give that one some thought?"

Hannah is even worse, because she breaks the silence in a creepier way: she sleepwalks. A week ago, she zombied her way into our room at 2:30 A.M. to ask, in that eerie, flat affect of the somnambulist, why we had decided to turn our home into a seafood restaurant and required her to become a waitress, thus ruining the birthday party she had planned for her pet zebra, Josephine. In our family, even being asleep isn't reason enough to stop talking.

In addition to these human distractions, my quiet is routinely disrupted by our useless pets. The family cat, Lucy, has a meow as loud as a barking dog, and frequently celebrates the witching hour by using my forehead as her ass throne. Our new dog is worse. Although Beauregard has absurdly long, floppy ears and jowls, the acoustic force of his ears and lips is his most astounding trick. Whenever he shakes his head, which he does each time I am about to enter a deep sleep, there is a prodigious flapping so rhythmic, resonant, and loud that it sounds uncannily like the beating of helicopter blades, as if a Huey were landing at the foot of the bed. Even when Beau is silent, which is rare, he is still deadly. His flatulence is so unspeakably toxic that when awakened by it, I find myself wishing he would shake his head some more, just to blast the stink away with his fanning ears and billowing lips.

All these disruptions to my quiet occur within the house, but the real acoustic trouble originates outside, where mice scurry along the windowsills and frequently succeed in gaining access to the walls. Once they breach the levee of the stucco exterior—which they can do through a gap as small as a quarter of an inch—

they delight in using their little claws and teeth to scratch and nibble at the drywall, which amplifies the scraping sound so much that as I lie in bed wide awake, I estimate the average mouse's weight at seventy pounds. Worse are the packrats, gifted climbers that in the absence of a handy cliff, scramble straight up the stucco exterior of the house, where they gnaw away at the soffits all night in an attempt to enter the attic. And the wind out here is huge, ripping down from the Sierra in winter and blasting out of the desert canyons as the Washoe Zephyr in summer.

It isn't only the wind that howls, but also the coyotes. What could be more enchanting than coyote song at night? Nature writers often croon about the experience of hearing the song of the pack, a transformative moment in which one is, apparently, obliged to feel an overwhelming spiritual bond with the nonhuman world. I, instead, nurture a deep bond with the fantasy of someday getting five hours of sleep. Coyote song is not at all as advertised. Their *chorus*, if we want to stretch a valorizing metaphor so far as to use that term, is less a sonorous howling than a chaotic cacophony of yips and yelps. I will consent to the word *chorus* only if I may stipulate that it is a chorus of inebriated third-graders. These selfish animals also refuse to yelp on my schedule, instead taking special pleasure in busting loose about the time I have finally rid myself of sleeptalking daughters and lip-flapping dogs.

Old Man Coyote is not alone out there. There are also the great horned owls, which, like the coyotes, do not often produce the pastoral night song we have been led to expect. Gentle hooting? Forget it. The signature, charismatic Hollywood hoot comprises about a fifth of their repertoire, while the remainder is an amalgamation of dissonant cries, whistles, shrieks, barks, and hisses. And may I be wrapped in rattlers if the raspy, piercing wail of an immature owl does not sound like a human baby screeching in agony because its little calf has been caught in the teeth of a steel leg trap.

Last Sunday, this immense desert night provided an unremitting sonic parade, a noisy nocturne in which the usual annoyances occurred serially over the course of what might otherwise have been a decent night's sleep. Sleeptalking kid, face-sitting cat, lip-flapping dog, scurrying mice, gnawing packrats, surging wind, yipping coyotes, and shrieking owls. Then, at 3:45 A.M., our chickens started clucking and squawking. Yet another of my ill-advised pastoral affectations, these hens are almost as useless as our pets. I feed them, clean their coop, keep them watered and warm, and generally enable their selfish, indolent lifestyle. They, in return, sometimes appear, perhaps, to be nearing the contemplation of, maybe, almost laying an egg, but then rarely follow through. Now, in addition to being unproductive, smelly, high-maintenance, and lazy, they were also being *loud*.

In a moment of pure frustration, I succumbed to that special kind of exhausted anger that arises when a desperate need for rest has been thwarted one too many times. In that moment, some biological imperative exerted itself, as a deeply repressed survival instinct eclipsed my last shred of equanimity and convinced me that sleep was worth fighting for. Enough was enough. If the chickens were blathering of their own accord, I intended to shut them up—for good, if necessary. If it was, instead, Old Man Coyote who was riling up the feathered imbeciles, then I intended to holler until I drove him into the night, where his racket could be drowned out by the roar of wind ripping through juniper and bitterbrush. Jumping out of bed, I grabbed the handle of my big, yellow flashlight and stomped angrily out into the desert, wearing only boxer shorts (lime green, with bright red ladybugs).

"*Shut up!*" I shouted into the night. "All y'all chickens, coyotes, owls, zip it! I moved out here to get some damned peace and quiet! *Shut . . . the . . . hell . . . UP!*"

As I cursed into the darkness, the darting beam of my flashlight caught a reflection in the sage. I now swung the beam back and panned slowly from right to left in search of whatever glint the light had caught. I froze as the beam suddenly locked on two greenish-yellow lasers that beamed back at me. In the penumbra of light glowing through the sage, I could now make out in silhouette the large, rounded face of a big cat.

I am not leery of rattlers or scorpions, but I am afraid of mountain lions, whose mule deer kills I have found atop my home mountain, and whose immense paw prints I discover inscribed like fierce hieroglyphics in the hardened caliche mud out on the flats near the canyon spring. As I stood barefoot and paralyzed, with the wind ripping through my boxers, I had a profound realization of exactly what sort of mistake I had just made. Not only was I unarmed, nearly naked, away from the house, and twenty feet from the eyes of a big cat that was not budging an inch, but I had just screamed at the King of the High Desert to shut the hell up. I had a momentary worry that in addition to being killed, I would also be featured in the Darwin Awards: "A Nevada man walked up to a mountain lion in the middle of the night in a remote area of the high desert and shouted at the big cat to 'shut the hell up.' The cat responded by attacking the man, killing him quickly with a vicious bite to the neck. The kill was silent, an irony the man did not live long enough to appreciate."

Trying not to focus on the comic potential of my looming evisceration, I backed away slowly, keeping the flashlight beam locked on those piercing eyes, expecting every moment that the big cat would spring toward me. But those greenish-yellow lasers remained unblinking, and, after what seemed an eternity, I backed against the door, slowly turned the knob behind my back while keeping those glowing eyes in sight, and eased into the house. Shutting the door quietly, I made several resolutions instantly. First, I would never, ever go outside again. Second, I would let Lucy the Desert Cat go outside immediately. Third, I would change my boxers as soon as possible. And fourth, I would snap on the exterior light in hopes of scoping the big cat. I quickly hit the switch and pressed my face to the window, cupping my hands around my forehead to reduce the glare. Slowly, calmly, out from the sagebrush walked a huge . . . bobcat.

Because bobcats can have a home range in excess of 100 miles and are elusive and retiring under any circumstances, the odds of getting a good look at one are vanishingly slim, even for a wild desert hillbilly like me. In a decade of living on Ranting Hill, I have enjoyed only a single glimpse of *Lynx rufus*, but now, out of nowhere on this chilly autumn night, came this desert ghost, strutting to center stage on its own well-lit catwalk. The bobcat strode gracefully across the desert flat beside our house and walked calmly beneath the girls' swing set. I was surprised at how long and cheetah-like its front legs appeared. The rear haunches were muscular and powerful, an adaptation for pouncing on big jackrabbits. The coloration of the thick fur was a wild combination of bars, dots, and bowed splotches that help to camouflage the animal as it stalks through the dappled scrub.

Before the bobcat receded into the darkness beyond the reach of the porch light, it paused just once, momentarily turning its head in my direction. Its face was beautiful, unmistakably lynx-like, with upright, black-tipped ears, and bright eyes, while the broad, curved flair of its whiskered cheeks made its head appear impossibly large. And then it was gone. Although it was only 4:00 A.M. I made myself a mug of strong java and sat in silence—at last, the magic of that long-sought, nourishing *silence*—looking out into the inky darkness, already treasuring a memory of the best night's sleep I never had.

AFTER TEN
THOUSAND YEARS

WANTING TO CLIMB one last mountain before winter shut down the high country until June, on Veterans Day I headed with my buddy Steve to Mount Augusta, a 10,000-foot peak in the remote Clan Alpine Range in west-central Nevada, just a few hours' drive east of Ranting Hill. From the summit of Augusta you gaze west across the vast alkali playa of Dixie Valley, into the precipitous eastern escarpment of the Stillwater Mountains, and then all the way to the Sierra Nevada crest above Lake Tahoe, more than 100 miles away. It was a perfect fall day in the mountains of the high desert: crisp, azure, bracing, and made sweeter by the knowledge that winter would soon swing the mountain's gates closed until late spring.

Although Steve and I had been out six or seven hours without seeing any people, we were not the first to pass this way. We found and left several glossy, black, obsidian arrowheads, which Steve examined for their percussion strike pattern and estimated were about ten thousand years old. On a steep, exposed traverse a few miles from the summit, we tracked a bighorn sheep in the snow before pausing to drink in the alpine light and expansive views.

"Steve," I said, "I'm gonna miss the high country when winter comes. This is the extreme, old-school, hard-core, all-out, straight-up, real-deal wilderness. . . ." At just this moment I was interrupted by a tremendous roaring out over Dixie playa, ten miles to the west.

"F-18s," Steve explained, as a distant pair of black dots glinted, banking into the sun.

I blinked once and then looked again to see the fighters slice through a high-mountain pass and roar directly at us with inconceivable speed. The planes hugged the rocky ground so closely that we instinctively fell to our chests and covered our ears with our palms as they shot over, and I could feel the ground vibrating so hard that for a moment it seemed that my ribs might pop off my sternum. As I glanced up from the rocks, squinting, I saw the chase plane rock its wings back and forth in greeting before suddenly flipping over and arcing, upside down, over the summit above us. In an instant, the fighters vanished, and an ocean of alpine silence engulfed the tunnel of thunder they had carved through the sky. I rose to my feet slowly, brushing gravel from my lips and beard.

"A pair of sixty-million-dollar arrowheads," Steve said, starting up the mountain again. "They can do almost Mach 2," he called back to me over his shoulder, "but they slowed down to about 700 miles an hour so they wouldn't burst our eardrums."

I stood frozen for a moment, still numb from this dramatic interruption of my mountain idyll. "You call this *wilderness*?" I shouted after Steve as he climbed into the sky without pausing to field my question. Sensing the waning of both the day and the season, I too pushed on toward the summit.

Not far from Mount Augusta is one of the loveliest high-elevation canyons in this part of Nevada: "GeeZee Canyon."

"GeeZee" is desert-rat longhand for "G. Z.," which is itself short-hand for "ground zero." It was here that, in the year I was born, a nuclear weapon was exploded. While nuclear tests in northern Nevada were few, more than nine hundred nuclear bombs were detonated at the Nevada Test Site in southern Nevada, which is a mere sixty-five miles from Las Vegas—a distance so short that those F-18s can cover it in about 200 seconds. Despite years of the federal government's unequivocal assurances of public safety, Nevada and Utah "downwinders" suffered and died from radiation-induced cancers in what many old folks in the Great Basin still view as a thermonuclear war waged upon their communities by their own government. As a plume of fallout dispersed across the Intermountain West, it blanketed farms and fields, ranches and schools, homes and towns, businesses and playgrounds. The devastating illnesses caused by radiation poisoning fell disproportionately on pregnant women and on children.

There is a deceptive transparency to the mountain air and light here in the high country of the Great Basin. As Steve and I climb silently toward the summit, I am struck by how much is visible from here: spectacularly beautiful, nearly uninhabited basin and range rippling out to the horizon, snow-clad peaks dotting the impossibly wide sky, vast sagebrush basins and alkali playas shimmering in the valleys below. But I am also struck by how much remains invisible, even from here. I am not able to see the Strontium-90 and Cesium-137, which are now as much a part of this place as granite and sage. Even looking through this remarkably clear, dry air, I cannot make out a single one of the six thousand people who, according to the National Cancer Institute, died as a result of radiation exposure from nuclear detonations in Nevada. It is not the view from this alpine peak that has sharpened my vision but the unforeseen appearance overhead of missile-bearing, supersonic fighter jets. I have entered a strange kind of patrolled wilderness in which fantasies of solitude are ruptured by the realization that we are always on the radar. Because today is Veterans Day, I find it impossible to forget the downwinders, for they too are veterans of the Cold War. A memory of these innocent victims is our only monument to the sacrifice they made for their nation on the invisible, nuclear battlefield of the American West.

Most of the time we Great Basinians tacitly agree to ignore the stubborn half-lives of radioactive isotopes in our land and the ineradicable memories of our people succumbing to cancer in small desert hospitals. We do so because we have dishes to wash, kids to dress, friends to help, mountains to climb. But while we work hard to forget, there is something besides fighter jets that reminds us that the West's nuclear history is not all in the past. Yucca Mountain, which is on the federal government's test site in southern Nevada, is the proposed repository for all of our nation's high-level nuclear waste—the most dangerous form of garbage our species has ever created. If some folks have their way, this waste will be transported by rail from more than a hundred sites in thirty-nine states, to be interred in a crypt beneath the Nevada desert. My intent here is not to revisit a decades-old debate about the risks and benefits of nuclear power generation. I only want to observe that one of the threads that connects Westerners to each other, and to Americans in other regions, is the glowing, invisible thread of the nuclear waste that may end up hidden beneath this magnificent desert. The same desert that has already been attacked with nine hundred nuclear weapons. The desert that is our home.

How long will obsidian last, I wonder? How long Strontium or Cesium? How long the memories of loved ones now gone? What is the half-life of this indescribable alpine light? We have summited Augusta, whose towering peak remains awash in history and time. Here my vision seems unusually clear, and as I gaze out across the terrible beauty of the Great Basin, I see clearly that we are downwinders all.

I once attended a hearing to learn more about the Nuclear Regulatory Commission's specific plans for nuclear waste storage at Yucca Mountain. The meeting was long and slow and consisted mostly of NRC scientists discussing in mind-numbing detail the technical design of the cask-and-cave burial system by which high-level radioactive waste could, they felt, be kept safe throughout the project's ten-thousand-year regulatory compliance period. Among the last to testify, however, was not a scientist but Corbin Harney, an elder of the Western Shoshone—who remain, to this day, an unconquered people. Corbin explained quietly that he opposed the plan because it was his ethical and spiritual duty to protect the land, its animals, and the people who would come after him.

"I understand completely," the NRC scientist replied, respectfully, "but we believe the storage casks will remain safe for ten thousand years."

"I understand completely," replied the old Shoshone, "but then what?"

WORDS AND CLOUDS

O UR CORNER OF THE western Great Basin is tucked into the rain shadow of the magnificent Sierra Nevada Mountains, which knock the bottom out of those big, wet storms that rise in the Pacific Ocean and cross California's Central Valley before pounding the Range of Light. Here, in Silver Hills, we average only seven inches of precipitation each year, while just up the mountain at Donner Pass (7,057 feet in elevation) the average is fifty-two inches, which falls in the form of thirty-four feet of snow—a detail that may be of special interest if you happen to be traveling by wagon train and do not have an appetite for "the other other white meat."

We do not see many clouds above Ranting Hill, where three hundred days of sunshine each year ensure that our passive-solar house remains self-heating until well into the cold nights we experience at this elevation. This winter has been especially clear and dry, making clouds in Silver Hills as scarce as city council members uncorrupted by real estate developers. In an era in which everything I thought was stored on my laptop is apparently kept in THE cloud, I find myself doubly troubled by these unbroken skies.

All this stunning high-desert cloudlessness has me thinking about clouds. Stratus. Cirrus. Cumulus. Nimbus. These are names so lovely that we might have named our daughters after them. It would, at least, have made hollering at the girls more entertaining: "Cirrus, take out the compost! Nimbus, collect those eggs!" Mostly, I am envisioning the signature cloud of the western Great Basin: the lenticular. A lenticular is a high-elevation cloud that is flat on the bottom and arched gracefully across its domed top. It resembles a flying saucer, for which it is sometimes mistaken—especially here in rural Nevada, where so few of us are wholly sane, and where we lead the nation in UFO sightings and alien abduction conspiracy theories. A lenticular forms when the moist air pouring over the Sierra hits the dry air rising from the desert floor, creating a cloud that is, essentially, a standing wave made visible. As that moist air sweeps over the top of the cloud, it vanishes into vapor, which is what makes the lenticular so special: it never leaves home as do other clouds, which drift across the sky. Lenticular clouds are the children of mountain and desert, and their essential nature is to perish precisely where they are born and shaped, an aerial analog of the dramatic ecotone below them.

In the disturbing absence of both altocumuli and the baseball season, my wandering writer's mind has also turned to the peculiar kind of cloud known as a "word cloud." As a graphic representation of words commonly used in any given text, a word cloud not only transforms language into visual art but also employs font size to represent the frequency of each word's use. So, for example, a word cloud of anything uttered by a political candidate would depict the word *FREEDOM* in 36-point type, while words such as *sustainable, endangered, poverty,* or *disarmament* would languish in wee 10-point. Thinking about word clouds caused me to wonder if, like actual clouds, they might function as messengers, as harbingers of fine weather or gathering storms. I wondered if a word cloud might form around a writer's sensibilities and values, not only exposing elements of style or voice but also revealing his secret dreams about this world as it is, or as it should be.

To test this proposition, I constructed a word cloud using the text of a tall stack of these "Rants from the Hill." The results of my lexical experiment were surprising and also a little disturbing, and at first it was tough to discern the silver lining of my vaguely ominous word cloud. The first thing I noticed is my obsession with local flora and fauna, which may confirm Eryn's suspicion that I am becoming a misanthropic curmudgeon. In fact, both *misanthrope* and *curmudgeon* appeared fairly prominently in the word cloud. Perhaps worse, it appears that I play favorites. Of the six native shrubs hereabouts, *sage, rabbitbrush, bitterbrush, ephedra,* and *desert peach* all received considerable air time, while *gooseberry* did not. For the record, gooseberry is a lovely little shrub in the currant family, rich with berries, excellent habitat for native birds and insects, and often as beautifully domed as a lenticular cloud. What could I have against gooseberry that I should snub it in this way? Could it have been a superstitious association with an actual goose that attacked me when I was a boy?

And why do I write so much more about *pronghorn* than *mule deer*? Might it be because the pronghorn was the sole antelope-like ungulate to survive the massive Pleistocene extinctions and has thus evolved in this place over the past twenty million years—or is it just cool to write about an animal that can run sixty miles per hour? Why do I apparently prefer *packrats* to *kangaroo rats*? Could it be because some fossil packrat midden sites in this area have seen continuous use for fifty thousand years, and that the ancient objects collected by packrats are indispensable to our understanding of long-term climate change? And what of my obvious bias for *jackrabbits* over *cottontails?* This must be attributable to the fact that cute, slow animals like the cottontail seem so out of place in this harsh, beautiful environment that any sensible person would join me in rooting for their predators—those elegant, vicious *owls* and *coyotes* whose names are so well represented in my Rant word cloud.

It seemed to me that my rationale for these preferences was perfectly defensible, but this self-assurance lasted only until the girls became involved in analysis of the word cloud. Hannah began by observing that neither she nor her little sister appeared anywhere in the word diagram. "That's because I so often call you my daughters, which is right here," I replied, pointing to a rather tiny *daughters* that appeared buried in the cloud. (Driven by remorse, I have since introduced their names more often throughout these essays.)

"Yeah, Dad, but *daughters* looks a lot smaller than *chainsaw* or *weed-whacker.*"

"Well, sure," I replied, "but a weed-whacker has a hundred and one uses. How many uses do you have?"

Wisely ignoring me, Hannah went on to point out that *daughters* also appeared smaller than *tractor*, *pickup*, *shotgun*, *snowshoes*, and *baseball.* Before I could mount a defense, Eryn chimed in that *beer* and even *IPA* were also larger than anybody in the family and that *whiskey* was among the most beloved words, even when *bourbon* and *rye* were also taken into consideration. Then came the coup de grâce: little Caroline noticed a word she could sound out and asked why *scat* also appeared larger than *daughters.* Sensing my impending loss in this battle of words, I beat a hasty retreat to my beer fridge to snag an IPA, quoting as I did from Twain: "Never argue with a fool; onlookers may not be able to tell the difference." This filched witticism wasn't a great fit, but I rationalized that writers, like children, must always have the last word. Besides, *fool* might now appear in my next Rant word cloud, which somehow seemed encouraging. (And if it didn't, I could always engage in word cloud seeding: *fool, fool, fool, fool, fool!*)

While the word cloud experiment offered a painful reminder of how rarely I win an argument (even with small children), it also revealed how endemic my prose is. In that sense, the cloud offered a salutary reminder that writing can function not only as a description of a local environment but also as an efflorescence of it. As what supergeeks would call "weighted keyword metadata," my Rant word cloud is literally created by desert diction, by words like *playa, caliche, arroyo, midden, aridity, pogonip, zephyr, foothill,* and *canyon*. In some profound sense, the words *desert* and *home* appear equally gigantic in my word cloud because, to me, they signify the same thing. The prominence of *wind, snow,* and *fire* must reflect the presence of those forces in this extreme landscape and in the wild imaginations of those of us who inhabit it—just as surely as must the absence of *rain clouds*. If, as a writer, I am less dreary than a stratus and less fluffy than a cumulus, neither am I as productive as a nimbus nor as lofty as a cirrus. Ultimately, my word cloud is a lexical and lyrical lenticular—something sculpted here in this montane-desert ecotone and always on the move in order to remain in place.

SINGING MOUNTAIN

WHEN WE FEEL THE SEASON begin to change from fall to winter up here on Ranting Hill, we get an itch to head out into the remote hinterlands that will soon be closed for the year by snow. It is as if we all sense that we will soon be huddled around our woodstove, happy to be holed up together but wondering if a few more trips out into the Great Basin might have eased the cabin fever just a bit.

With the bittersweet turning of the season looming, our family piled into the truck and headed east from Ranting Hill, speeding along highway 50, the officially designated "Loneliest Road in America," through boulder-choked mountain passes and across vast alkali basins on our way to a remarkable place called Sand Mountain, where we arrived in the chill of an early November afternoon. Sand Mountain is a single, winding sand dune, three miles long and a mile wide. This megadune rises among rocky desert mountains that are so much darker in color and so geologically dissimilar from it as to make this dramatic, white dune appear absolutely surreal. Unlike a beach dune, which is clearly part of its home landscape, Sand Mountain is so unique as to appear completely alien.

To appreciate Sand Mountain requires a leap of imagination. Fifteen thousand years ago the Sierra Nevada Mountains were heavily glaciated, but a subsequent warming trend began to melt the glaciers, dumping enough water down the eastern Sierra to fill immense expanses of the Great Basin with massive inland lakes. Ancient Lake Lahontan, whose depth reached 800 feet, once extended across much of present-day northern Nevada and covered more than 8,000 square miles of this now-desiccated landscape. Toward the end of the Pleistocene, the giant lake began to dry up, and four thousand years ago it had contracted so far as to expose the spot where Sand Mountain now rises. As the massive, retreating glaciers scoured the Sierra Nevada, they ground off flakes and pebbles of granite, which were further degraded as they tumbled down rivers and were borne out into the Great Basin.

At the delta of the Walker River near Shurz, Nevada (pop. 658)—where the Ghost Dance prophet Wovoka lies buried in a Paiute graveyard—this granitic sand accumulates in a place that is sanctified by wind. Here, the prevailing Southwesterlies swoop down and gather up this glacier-ground and river-trundled sand, lifting it high into the air and carrying it across the open desert more than thirty miles, where the flanks of the Stillwater Mountains at last slow the winds, causing them to drop their payload of Sierra sand in this enchanted spot. Over time, this weird, lovely pile of sand has grown to 600 feet in height, making Sand Mountain one of the tallest dunes in North America. This is the story of the birth of Sand Mountain, which is still being born.

Sand Mountain is one of only thirty-five dunes on the planet that knows how to sing. A "singing dune" consists of what is called singing, whistling, or even barking sand—sand that is capable of making a roaring or booming sound that has also been described as a hollow rustle. Although scientists debate precisely how the sound is created, it is associated with the rate of collision in the shear band where avalanching sand on a steep face makes contact with static sand below. Only dunes in warm, dry climates are capable of song, and even then they are silent, unless consisting of perfectly clean sand with silica-based grains of a specific and nearly uniform size and shape. When Sand Mountain sings, it produces a unique note of between sixty and 105 hertz. Northern Paiute and Western Shoshone people have long honored this distinctive song, which they attribute to Kwansee, their ancient tribal benefactor, who lies buried beneath the dune and who sings for his lost love.

When Eryn, the girls, and I arrived at Sand Mountain, the sun was already dropping into the horizon clouds. Although it was cold and windy, we decided to try for the summit ridge of the dune before nightfall, clambering first up the flank of the mountain and then along one of its winding knife ridges, straight into the sky. Each step pushed a small avalanche of sand behind us, making the climb so challenging that we grown-ups adopted the technique that Hannah and Caroline had instinctively used from the start: scrambling upward on all fours. After the better part of an hour of this odd clambering we reached the summit, which turned out to be a single ridge of sand so incredibly narrow that we all straddled it, as if riding horseback, in order to keep from sliding down the even more precipitous incline on its far side. From this precarious position we had a sweeping view along the sinuous, dragon-backed ridge of the giant dune, down to the expansive playa below, and then out to the vast, rippling basin and range country beyond.

From our perch we discerned no life apart from ourselves, but I am aware of one secret life that is lived here, and here alone. The Sand Mountain blue butterfly (*Euphilotes pallescens arenamontana*) is a lovely little sister in the family *Lycaenidae*, the gossamer-winged butterflies. It lives nowhere on earth save for this one barren, striking place. The little blue's existence is restricted to Sand Mountain because its survival depends entirely on Kearney buckwheat (*Eriogonum nummulare*), a local plant that is the sole food source for its larvae. The Sand Mountain blue spends its entire life within 200 feet of its host plant, and that life consists of only a single, beautiful week. We too often forget how much beauty a week can produce. The little blue butterfly is here because of the buckwheat, which is here because of the dune, which is here because a special wind delivered the harvest of a long-vanished glacier that patiently turned a mountain of stone into one of sand.

From the top of Sand Mountain we have something more than a view; we have a prospect. *Prospect*, a word not associated with mining until the 1840s, has been used since the early fifteenth century to describe the "act of looking into the distance." By the early sixteenth century, the word also connoted an "extensive view of the landscape," and since the early seventeenth century, its meaning has expanded to reference a psychological outlook, a "mental view or survey." At its Latin root, *prospect* implies a vantage from which to look ahead of oneself into both space and time (*pro* means "forward"). A prospect is a view of the land, of oneself, and also of what is yet to come. What was the prospect from the windy, knife-ridged summit of Sand Mountain? Night descending on endless salt flats. The Great Basin rolling out to the distant future. Our beautiful daughters gazing from the spine of the world toward an infinite horizon.

The desert darkness began its long fall, and the time had come to descend Sand Mountain. We agreed with the girls' suggestion that we should all head downhill in the most exciting way possible: by rolling. We lay down laterally along the ridge, pulled our stocking caps down firmly, tucked our arms in tightly against our bodies, and then held our breath and let gravity take over. The pitch was surprisingly steep, and we gained speed so quickly that we were soon blasted out of a rolling position and into a wild tumble down the face of the dune. The sand cascaded away before us, as the world spun and spun, and the four of us fell together, the mountain falling gently with us.

When we reached the bottom, I looked up, still dizzy, to see Caroline, her face and hair completely covered in sand, pumping her fists above her head. "That was *magnifulous!*" she shouted.

It was a peaceful drive home through the desert night, as we cruised quietly toward Venus by threading through a fantastic, otherworldly, starlit landscape. Now back on Ranting Hill, with Eryn and the girls fast asleep, I am still waiting for my imagination to return from Sand Mountain. Through this moonless desert darkness I contemplate a 600-foot-tall dune of white sand that was brought to its place one grain at a time over the winding course of four millennia. It is a graceful heap of the powdered bones of the Sierra Nevada, pulverized by glaciers, tumbled in rivers, lifted by wind, carried aloft to a new home. Like its rare blue butterfly, this mountain can exist in only one place, where the conditions necessary for its existence conspire to make its unreal beauty not only possible but necessary and inevitable. And yet the mountain changes shape every year and every hour. It flows, like the currents of wind and water that formed it. Like an advancing or retreating glacier. Like time, which moves mountains.

My desert dream is to be as endemic as Sand Mountain and its petite blue, but the shifting sands that turn the years remind me that we are being constantly resculpted by movement and change. *Tempus fugit, ergo carpe diem.* Because even mountains flow, I am too old not to roll down them with my children.

TOWERING CELL TREES

THE OTHER DAY, while driving down from the Sierra Nevada into the Great Basin on my way home to Ranting Hill, I noticed next to the local volunteer fire station one of those cell phone towers that is disguised to look like a tree—in this case, a vaguely ponderosa-ish pine. What strikes me as most odd about these cell towers costumed as trees is that they do not much resemble trees, at least not to anyone who paid any attention to real trees in the first place. You get the sense that the designers of these bizarre, fake trees are under the illusion that the towers actually look like real trees, which is both cute and somehow pathetic.

Simply by virtue of scale, this issue of what cell towers look like is more significant than you might think. There are almost seven billion mobile phones in the world, 328 million of which are in the United States, which means that we have more cell phones than people in America, even if you count the infants—which is probably wise, since babies will be using smartphones soon enough. This level of saturation necessitates a lot of towers: about two hundred fifty thousand in the United States alone, which adds up to a lot of ugly crap on hilltops and ridgelines. Because the range of a cell tower isn't much above twenty miles, even when those hills and ridges are not in the way, and because the number of towers is proportional to the number of users, we need to build more towers every day—towers that are most effective when installed in visually prominent places.

It makes sense, then, that we entrepreneurial Americans would find a way to make a virtue of necessity and sell not only cell towers but also ways of disguising them. The tower-as-tree innovation was the brainchild of Tucson-based Larson Camouflage, which pioneered the "mono-pine" back in 1992 and has since earned the dubious distinction of being "a leader in the concealment industry." Larson has figured out how to turn cell towers into a wide range of cultural and architectural objects, from water towers, grain silos, and gas station signs to streetlights, flagpoles, and chimneys. My favorite of these obfuscations is the disguising of a cell tower as a church steeple—an appealing business proposition, since many local building codes permit churches an exception to a structure's maximum allowable height. It is even the case that some churches without steeples are now building them solely to accommodate cell towers. This can generate a handsome income in leasing fees, which average forty-five thousand dollars per year but in some places run as high as a half-million bucks. Any cash-strapped congregation might look up to its steeple and find that its prayers have been answered.

While I enjoy contemplating the cultural significance of the fact that some folks who gaze up at a church steeple in prayer are actually supplicating a microwave radiation-emitting cell phone tower, I am even more interested in the ambitious attempt to disguise towers as natural objects. In addition to the artificial pine-tower (which is available in an impressive variety of "branch-density options"), Larson offers tower concealment in the form of several other "species," including the palm (available with or without "decorative cut-frond pineapple"), cypress, elm, and even saguaro cactus, which features "scars, woodpecker holes and thousands of painted needles [to] enhance the realism." According to the Larson website, "even the birds can't tell the difference." Just don't tell that to the Gila woodpeckers, white-winged doves, and house finches that feed on the giant cactus's pulp, or the two kinds of bats that pollinate its flowers, or the many other species that thrive on and around these remarkable cacti—that is, when they aren't made of plastic. The same may be said of pine, cypress, and elm, each of which is a vital host plant to an extensive, interdependent community of species.

It is not entirely fair of me to pick on these invasive, exotic fake trees as being profoundly unnatural interventions into the landscape. After all, the question is not whether a fake tree is better than a real tree but whether a fake tree is better than an exposed cell tower. But even here the question is more difficult than it appears. First of all, there is the troubling fact that the structure, color, shape, and stiffness of these decoys usually give them away, which makes the claim of "concealment" arguable. I also wonder about the longevity of these microwave "trees." Not far from the fake ponderosa pine, I noticed near the fire station a stand of actual ponderosas, many of which will live to be three hundred years old. What are the odds that the fake will still be in decent shape after three centuries, and what sprucing up (sorry for the pun) might it require in the meantime? In what landfill will we bury this giant plastic thing when its inorganic "life" has run its course?

Then there's the troubling fact that a decent fake-tower tree runs a cool hundred fifty thousand dollars, which represents an exorbitant opportunity cost in a world where the same amount of dough will pay for the planting of around one hundred fifty thousand trees as part of a forest habitat rehabilitation project. And every one of those one hundred fifty thousand unplanted trees would have enriched soils, reduced erosion, supported other species, and sequestered hundreds of metric tons of carbon, all while bearing an uncanny resemblance to trees. Even the birds would be able to tell the difference.

I realize that this kind of self-righteous, tree-hugging sermonizing dodges the central issue, which is that cell phone towers are just plain ugly. So, from my perch on Ranting Hill, I have a few alternatives to propose. The first is to leave the naked masts of the towers exposed but adorn them with large signs that read "This Aesthetic Abomination Is Made Necessary by Your Uncontrollable Desire to Post Meaningless Status Updates." An alternative in the same spirit would be to make all the cell towers into fake trees but add signs saying "This Ineffective Obfuscation Cost Three Times the US Median Family Income." Or, if that's too wonky, we could go with "Sixteen Million American Children Live in Poverty but We Can Afford This Unconvincing Fake." Or maybe every time we install a new cell tower we should just retrofit all the nearby real trees to look like cell towers so the cell tower will simply blend in.

My best idea, though, is that we give up on the fake trees entirely and make the cell towers look like other objects. Admitting that a powerful nexus of technology and commerce is profoundly altering our local landscapes, I say it is about time we at least got a laugh out of it. Imagine seeing a 100-foot-tall banana, fork, ground squirrel, thumb, or baseball bat rising among the stately ponderosas. What if we gave my friend, the artist, a fifty-thousand-dollar grant to spend a year turning our local cell phone tower into whatever she could imagine? My guess is that we would end up with a 100-foot-tall giraffe's head—probably wearing a Giants ball cap. It wouldn't look like a ponderosa, but neither does the fake ponderosa, and at least the giant giraffe would make my daughters smile. And this fifty-thousand-dollar work of art would have the added advantage of being a reminder that we saved one hundred thousand dollars that we could use for something *really* crazy, like planting real trees.

RANTOSAURUS SILVERHILLSII

L AST SATURDAY, around noon, I was feeling desperate for more time alone when Hannah and Caroline asked if I was finally ready to play with them. I had been making excuses all morning, explaining that I needed to get Beauregard out for a hike, that I had to split some wood, that it was important for me to haul rock to riprap a drainage trench I had recut with the backhoe. In truth, these chores were an excuse to drink beer, listen to good blues, and have some time to sift the week's detritus through my partially clogged noggin filter.

"It occurs to me that you girls haven't watched enough TV today," I replied, brew in hand. "Let me recommend *Scooby-Doo*. Facilitates cerebral development. Worked for me, anyhow. Besides, your teachers aren't going to help you learn important words like 'Zoinks' and 'Jinkies.' Why don't you meddling kids go fire up a couple of episodes?"

At just that moment, Eryn stepped around the corner of the house, frowning at her irresponsible husband. "*Ruh-roh*," I muttered, changing my tune. "Girls, much as I hate to deprive you of Scooby, let's go play. What did you have in mind?"

"Let's build something ginormous!" exclaimed Caroline.

"I think we should build a gigantic one of *those*," said Hannah, pointing at the label on my beer bottle. "What *is* that thing, Dad?" I had been drinking the best beer brewed in the Truckee Meadows: an Ichthyosaur IPA from Great Basin Brewing—a barleypop fondly called an "Icky" by all brewfully inclined western Great Basinians.

"That, my dear, is an Ichthyosaur. It was a giant marine reptile that swam around Silver Hills when this place was beneath the ocean a couple hundred million years ago. It also happens to be the state fossil of Nevada." At first the girls didn't believe me that states have their own representative fossils. "Yup," I continued, "but most of them aren't as cool as ours. Arizona's is petrified wood. Lame. In Tennessee, it's the bivalve. Even lamer. In Connecticut, dinosaur tracks. Lamest of all, because the state fossil of Massachusetts was already dinosaur tracks. But Nevada has a big old sea lizard. We rock!" I hoisted the bottle in cheers and used my free hand to fist-bump with the girls.

With that, Caroline raised both puny arms above her head and shouted, "Let's build a giant Itchy-sore!"

Hannah asked immediately what we would build it out of, and I confess that the prospect of constructing a giant sea lizard registered with me as the ten-thousandth time I had felt myself inadequate to a task that was, suddenly, very important to my kids.

"How about firewood?" Eryn suggested.

I grinned in reply. "That, my friend, is genius. Let's do it! Girls, y'all go make a quick sketch of a sea monster, and I'll hook up the trailer and get your work gloves."

Twenty minutes later I had us ready to haul wood, and the girls had drawn a prototype marine reptile. In addition to having

Rantosaurus Silverhillsii   / 159

a serpentine shape that would make it look like it was wriggling through the swells of this sagebrush ocean, it would also have a series of big humps, each larger than the last, as we built our way toward the head. Eryn added a creative twist: if we could construct the spine of our sea beast with high humps but low saddles in between, a good snow would bury the arches and reveal the humps, making it appear that our marine reptile was swimming through a frothy ocean of fresh powder.

In order to keep packrats from colonizing too close to our house (we've had *Neotoma cinerea*, that furry wonder, nesting in the crawl space beneath the floors more than once), we keep the woodpile a quarter mile down our half-mile-long driveway. The girls pulled on their gloves and climbed into my small utility trailer, and we bounced down to the woodpile and started loading bucked juniper, pinyon, and ponderosa, a little Doug and white fir mixed in. Returning to the house, we selected a flat area near the garage and began laying out the logs, starting at the tail and, at first, using only a single-log construction so as to establish the shape of our giant reptile. As we did, Eryn sat nearby in a lawn chair, reading about Ichthyosaurs to the girls from something she had searched up on her phone.

"Ichthyosaurs lived from 245 to 90 million years ago and were widely distributed around the globe," she reported. "Early Triassic to Late Cretaceous. They evolved from a group of unidentified land reptiles that, at some point, moved back into the sea. The name *Ichthyosaur* is from the Greek, meaning 'fish lizard.' Although they swam like fish and looked a lot like fish, they were reptiles. The fact that they developed a lot of fishlike parts is called 'convergent evolution.' That means that although fish and Ickys are totally unrelated, they developed similar kinds of fins, because it's just useful to have fins if you want to swim."

The girls asked some follow-up questions, decided to add an

improvised fin-log to each of the monster's humps, and paused for water a few times. But mainly they just worked at stacking the wood along the spine of their giant reptile, which began to take shape, rising from the desert floor in a very satisfying way.

"Ickys averaged six to thirteen feet long, but some were much larger," Eryn continued. "The largest Ichthyosaur fossils ever discovered, which were almost fifty feet long, were found in . . . wait for it . . ."

"*Nevada!*" Hannah shouted. Eryn gave her a wide smile and a thumbs-up.

Because our sea lizard was so long and sinuous, its body swallowed up a surprising amount of wood, and so we fetched a second trailer load and, eventually, a third. By the time the third load was placed along the rising, humped spine of our giant reptile, it was late afternoon and the already low winter sun was dropping fast. But the kids refused to quit, begging me to fashion a big reptile head, which was the only thing missing from what had become a truly respectable cordwood sea monster. Caroline and Hannah's desert ocean lizard now wriggled impressively across the sand and had imposing humps, the largest of which rose a full five feet from the ground.

Knowing I had so little time before dark and that my lack of artistic ability would be a serious liability even under better circumstances, I decided to attach whatever dragony-looking stuff I could quickly find nearby. Parenting, like jazz, is the art of improvisation. I first took a twisted length of juniper branch and stuck it into the front hump to suggest a neck. Then, I grabbed my cordless drill from the garage and attached a piece of old barnboard to the end of the neck. From a trashcan full of scrap wood I salvaged two small log-ends, which I repurposed as eyes, attaching them hastily to the barnboard brow with old deck screws. I screwed much smaller log-ends onto the eyes to resemble pupils. I then bored holes down each side of the neck, and into them I jammed branches that I lopped from the trunk of last year's pinyon pine Christmas tree, which was still lying on the ground not far from the woodpile. Finally, I used my chainsaw to cut a curved flange of root from a big pine stump, and I inverted it and popped it onto the forehead as an improvised horn.

Finishing my work just at dusk, I popped another Icky and stepped back to consider what redneck art had wrought. So awful were the results of my effort that I momentarily wished I lived in Arizona, where I would presumably have been asked by my kids to make a state fossil that looked like petrified wood. ("Here's a piece of wood," I'd say. "Now just pretend that it's actually a rock.") Our giant reptile's head left the impression of a gene-splicing experiment gone terribly wrong. Rather than resembling the noble marine reptile that had been the terror of ancient seas, the skull of this monster looked like it belonged to a cross between a giant lamprey eel, a misshapen desert unicorn, and an inebriated reindeer. In addition to being the art of improvisation, I had long since come to view parenting as the constant condition of having to admit publicly one's numberless shortcomings. I felt ashamed that at the end of the girls' remarkable wood sculpture, I had produced a head so abominably bad as to turn the wonderful beast into a lamentable sort of Jurassic jackalope.

"Well, girls, my work here is done. Thanks to me, your awesomely cool marine reptile does not, in fact, look like an Ichthyosaur. Not in the least. I'm really sorry about that."

"That's OK, Daddy," Caroline offered. "Our monster doesn't have to be any certain kind, so long as we made it ourselves. And it really *is* awesome. This guy can just be our own special made-up kind of desert sea monster."

Hannah was even more consoling. "Dad, you spent all afternoon building this with us, which is double awesome. Why don't you write a Rant about our big lizard? Then, we can just forget about the whole Icky thing and call him 'Rantosaurus'!"

As Caroline nodded in agreement, I found myself thinking that a kid's universe is not only more imaginative than the grown-up world, but also more humane. Millions of years ago, this desert had been ocean, and someday it might be ocean once again. But for one small, already disappearing moment in the life of this place, I was the flawed father of understanding children and the co-creator of a giant desert sea monster. It would be foolish to wish for more.

"OK, y'all. Rantosaurus it is. *Rantosaurus silverhillsii*. Not only rare, but unique. Nothing like it anywhere in the world."

By now Eryn had come out to "admire my art," as she put it with a grin, and to call us in for supper. "It looks pretty fierce," she said. "What do you want it to protect us from? I'd like to be protected from rattlers in the garage and Beauregard slobbering on my work clothes. How about you, Bubba?"

I took one more swig of the delicious Icky IPA. "Light beer, illegal off-roaders, climate-change deniers, and county commissioners. Not necessarily in that order. Hannah, how about you?"

"OK, let's see. Mountain lions and Brussels sprouts. Caroline, how about you?"

"Dog poop. And when teachers get mad. I want Rantosaurus to just gobble up mad teachers."

"I think that's a fine idea, sweetie," I said, in a tone of sincere approval.

Caroline had one last question. "Dad, I know our sea monster isn't really an Icky, but is it as big as one—as big as one of those big Nevada ones, I mean?"

"Let's find out," I said, taking her small hand in mine. We then paced off the length of our monster, starting at the head, which towered over her little body, and tracing the curves of its gracefully winding spine until we reached the tip of the tail. "Well, honey, your Rantosaurus is about forty feet long, which is impressive, but Mom read that the whopper Nevada ichthyosaurs were almost fifty feet long. Are you disappointed?"

"Naaw," she replied without hesitation. "He'll keep growing, and next winter, when we build him again, he'll be even bigger."

HILLBILLY CYBORG

I HAVE NEVER LIKED COWS ONE BIT. I know cattle come off looking pretty good in Hollywood glamorizations of drives on the Western trail, and cows are supposed to be cute when they appear in the form of your great aunt's Holstein knickknack collection, but the plain fact is that cows are lazy, unattractive, smelly, ill-mannered, and can't be trusted. I have made close observations of cattle out on the BLM land here in Silver Hills, and I do not like what I see. It is tough to manage much admiration for an animal that lumbers back and forth on the same path all day, and I am not impressed by bovine intelligence when I see fat cows standing in the only spring in this valley, plopping huge butt pies into the sparkling water, and then bending forward to lap that water up, as if they have somehow improved its flavor.

Without launching an ecogeek polemic here, it may be enough to say that cattle can be hard on wild lands, causing erosion, dispersing invasive plants, destroying riparian habitat, and displacing native wildlife. Thirty years ago, while backpacking the Escalante

Canyons in southern Utah, I was so heartbroken by the environmental damage caused by cattle grazing that I resolved, in that moment, to end my complicity by withdrawing from the hamburger economy, and I have not eaten beef since. And don't forget that the release of methane gas by bovines contributes to global climate change. Next time you see the pitiable image of a stranded polar bear adrift on a chunk of floating ice, think cow farts.

This account of my dislike of cattle makes it sound entirely principled. In truth, my main objection to cows is that they appear crazy-eyed and drunk. Out on the range they look as if they are always about to fall over, as if they just tossed back a five-gallon-bucket shot of tequila that hasn't quite hit them yet but will momentarily. Think, by comparison, of the quickness, agility, and attentiveness of wild things—how coyote, pronghorn, rattler, and harrier are like the string of an instrument that millions of years of evolutionary fine-tuning has tightened to perfect pitch. There is no graceless motion or lapse in concentration, let alone giant tequila shots or pooping in their own water source.

When I look into the eyes of cows, by contrast, they gaze back with a disturbing blankness that seems to say, "I might kill you, or you might kill me, or I might just stand here and fart, and it's all the same to me." This is not the kind of calculus I want to see revealed in the eyes of a fellow mammal. And while these spindly legged, dung-encrusted knuckleheads hardly look threatening, I can't help picturing the running of the bulls in Pamplona, Spain—or Elko, Nevada, where we continue the venerable, Old World Basque Country tradition of getting drunk and daring angry cows to kill us—and I wonder how long it would take one of these cranky fat boys to go from bore to gore, from trying lazily to bum tequila off me to turning me into a ranting shish kebab. I have looked deep into the black hole of those bovine eyes and have lived to tell the chilling tale: There is no there there. It is pure existential void.

When I was in seventh grade, a big kid named Billy Green, who had failed the fifth and sixth grades a number of times and was thus approximately twenty years old at the time, punched me in the face as payback for my having accidentally hit him with a softball during recess. I handled this difficult moment with my usual courage and aplomb, by crying like a baby, spouting blood, and blubbering helplessly, "Billy, you're . . . you're going to have to pay the doctor bill!"

I doubt I appeared very threatening, since several of my front teeth were, at that moment, protruding through a gash in my lower lip. Ever since that time, I've had problems with those teeth, and recently I received the troubling news that the abused choppers would have to be yanked out, and that deterioration in my jaw would have to be remedied with a bone graft. Speaking as a person who would rather be punched in the face by Billy Green every single day than sit in a dentist's chair for thirty minutes, I respond poorly to terms like "surgery," "extraction," or "implant," and least of all did I welcome the idea of a "bone graft." My situation went from bad to worse when I asked my nerdy oral surgeon where he would harvest the bone that would be used in the graft. His disturbingly enthusiastic reply was, "From a cow!"

As you might imagine, this news caused me genuine consternation. A perfectly intelligent man of substantial professional training and experience was casually proposing that he should pull teeth out of my head and replace part of my jaw with freeze-dried cow bone. Was this a cruel joke? Looking up helplessly from the chair, I carefully explained to the oral surgeon all about the hollow eyes and the tequila shots and the iceberg-thawing flatulence, and I begged him to perform the operation using bone from a chimpanzee, armadillo, or wallaby. He replied calmly that it had to be cow, and added, reassuringly, "Oh, and don't worry about contracting mad cow disease from this."

"Thanks a bunch," I said, drooling prodigiously onto my clip-on bib. "I wasn't worried about that at all . . . until now."

Yesterday I went in for my operation, which I don't have the stomach to relate in detail. When I was placed in the dreaded chair—a memory that already feels dreamlike and surreal—the radio was tuned, unhappily, to our local country station, KBULL, which happened at that moment to be twanging out Johnny Cash's cover of "Ghost Riders in the Sky," a terrifying ballad about "a mighty herd of red-eyed cows" whose "brands were still on fire" and whose "hooves were made of steel." The surgeon revved up the drill just as the Man in Black described the "bolt of fear" that went through him as the demonic cattle began their deadly stampede. I do not remember much after that, and the fragments I do recall were processed through the distorted filter of hallucinogenic fear: a synesthetic blending of the sound of drills, the feeling of splattering water, the metallic taste of blood, the charred smell of grinding bone, and the horrific imagination of rising from the chair to look in the mirror and discover that my head had been fully transformed into that of a cow.

I survived the procedure, but it is certain that I will never be the same again, for part of my jaw is now built of the bones of my enemy. Once fully human, I am now a hillbilly cyborg, part man and part cow. Like Captain Ahab, whose prosthetic leg was crafted from whalebone, if I continue to bad-mouth cows, I will have to do it with a mouth that is part cow. Perhaps my own epic account of man and monster will begin like Melville's, but with this opening line: "Call me Cabeza de Vaca."

I search my imagination for some ennobling analog for my bizarre transformation. As a kid who watched too much TV during the late 1970s, I remember *The Six Million Dollar Man*, in which a cool, handsome astronaut who sustains serious injuries is rebuilt with cutting-edge technology that makes him stronger, faster, and even better-looking. And six million dollars is approximately what this oral surgery has cost me. I run some quick numbers on the procedure and determine that the amount of money I have paid to have a few milligrams of cow bone stuck into my head would have bought 800 pounds of fresh ground beef—or, perhaps better, a half dozen full-grown steers that I could keep on the back forty, in case I need additional cow bone for future operations. I also learned that the cash spent on my smidgen of cow bone would have gone a long way toward buying an entire cobalt-chrome hip joint, which makes me wonder if it would have been a better value to skip the cow and simply rebuild my jaw using a prosthetic hip.

I am no handsome astronaut, and I am neither stronger nor faster than before I raided my kids' college fund to become a cow head. But at least I do not eat cows, which, under my new circumstances, would seem rather like a person who had received a heart transplant from a pig waking up the morning after the operation to scarf down a plate of bacon. I try to make light of my dental misery, telling Hannah and Caroline jokes that I have crafted for the occasion: "What happened to the cow whose bones are in Daddy's face? Nobody's herd!" But beneath this strained humor, my relationship to nonhuman nature seems more visceral and intimate than ever before. I still distrust cows, but now, when I meet them out on the BLM, I detect a strange kinship. Somehow they look at me a little differently, as if to ask, "Hey, smart-ass, where would you be without us?" And when I brush my teeth in the morning, I sometimes notice an irrational, vacant, slightly insane look in my own dark eyes, as if my bovinification has led me closer to the profound metaphysical question being asked each day by cows everywhere: *Got tequila?*

OUT ON MISFITS FLAT

THE QUINTESSENTIAL NEVADA film is John Huston's 1961 picture *The Misfits*, starring Marilyn Monroe, Clark Gable, and Montgomery Clift. The movie had its origin in playwright Arthur Miller's trip to Nevada in 1956. While doing his mandatory six-week Nevada residency in order to divorce his first wife so he could marry Marilyn Monroe, Miller closely observed the landscapes and people of Nevada, even witnessing a wild horse roundup out on the Smoke Creek Desert. He documented his Nevada experience in the short story "The Misfits," which appeared in *Esquire* magazine in October 1957, and which he subsequently rewrote as a screenplay he described as a "valentine" for Monroe, for whom he created the starring role of Roslyn Tabor.

The plot of this dark film might be summarized as follows: Roslyn, a fragile, lost woman seeking a divorce, comes to Reno, where she meets three lost men—three different sorts of washed-up cowboys—each of whom is also in escape mode and all of whom soon fall in love with her. This odd crew remains impressively drunk most of the time. At last, they head out into the desert to hunt wild mustangs in a roundup so violent and tragic as to compel the realization that the values of the Old West, now gone forever, have been replaced by nothing but uncertainty, instability, and loneliness.

Sound fun? The story gets better. In addition to the production of *The Misfits* being an over-budget and behind-schedule nightmare of emotional volatility, psychological pressure, drug addiction, alcoholism, and excessive gambling on the part of cast and crew alike, the picture now has an overhyped but irresistible reputation for having destroyed many of the people associated with it. The newly minted, highly publicized Miller-Monroe marriage imploded during the making of the film, as Monroe spiraled downward into narcotics addiction. Gable, who at age fifty-nine insisted on doing many of his own stunts, said of Monroe on the last day of shooting, "I'm glad this picture's finished. She damn near gave me a heart attack." The next day, he suffered a heart attack; ten days later he was dead. *The Misfits* was also the final film for Monroe, who died of a probable suicide in the summer of 1962. She was only thirty-six. Monty Clift survived a few years longer than his costars, but the film plays a strange role in his demise as well. *The Misfits* was on television on the evening of July 22, 1966. Asked by his partner if he wanted to watch it, Clift headed off to bed with a curt reply: "Absolutely not." Those were his last words. By morning he was dead.

I call *The Misfits* the quintessential Nevada film because it so powerfully dramatizes the restlessness and uncertainty of whatever the New West is and is still becoming. Miller insightfully described Nevada as a fascinating, alien place inhabited by people who had in common only that they had come here to "escape something somewhere." As Miller observed decades later, "In a way they were free people, but they were unfree in the sense that there was an unrequited longing for something they couldn't name." "Misfits" are these free yet unfree people who remain trapped between a troubled past and an uncertain future, between the erasure of the iconography of independence associated with the Old West and the radical mobility and instability of the New West. They have managed to escape the encumbrances and responsibilities that burden most of us, but in severing those ties they have also become unmoored, set adrift in the chartless immensity of a shoreless sagebrush ocean.

The landscape of the Great Basin is crucial to the film's thematic force and visual aesthetic. Miller was fascinated by the fact that in this wild desert, "the people were so little and the landscape was so enormous." "They were practically little dots, and you felt that with them," he observed. "They were like specks of dust across the road." Speaking as one of those specks, I agree that the existential reality of life in the Great Basin is a matter of scale—both a temporal and spatial scale within which the illimitable openness of the big empty offers a constant reminder of our own inconsequentiality. This is the realization the unhomed characters in *The Misfits* seek desperately to avoid but must ultimately face.

Crucial to the film is the place where Roslyn and the three men finally confront this loss: a remote playa—what we call the vast alkali flats in the basins between desert mountains—that is the site of the roundup of wild horses that so dramatically concludes the picture. It is a painful scene in which the tools of the New West (an airplane and a truck) are used to capture six wild mustangs, which are to be sold for a pittance and unheroically rendered into dog food. Although the horses are ultimately released after Roslyn has a breakdown while witnessing their cruel treatment, it is clear that the Old West is headed for the meat grinder and that no one has the slightest idea what to do about it—or how they will possibly endure whatever might come next.

As an admirer of this desperate film, and as a man desperate for an excuse to skip work and go hoofing in the desert, I decided to try to find the spot where this dark crescendo of *The Misfits* was shot. After some research, I discovered that the mustanging scene had not been filmed on the Smoke Creek Desert, as some sources suggested, but instead on a playa near the waterless wide spot of Stagecoach, down in Lyon County. Unlike roughly 85 percent of Nevada, this playa turned out to be private land, which meant that an unauthorized visit could be hazardous to my health. Who in hell owns their own desert?

Eventually, I tracked down the owner, a guy named Lester, who agreed to meet me in Carson City to tell some stories and give me access to "Misfits Flat," which is what this unnamed desert playa came to be called after it was fatally associated with Miller and Huston, Monroe and Gable. Before leaving Ranting Hill for Carson Valley, I invited my friend Cheryll to ride shotgun. She's an expert on Nevada literature and has a passion for the Huston film; even more important, she wears a bright-red snowsuit that looks cool out on playas, where the bone-white immensity of snow and sand constantly threatens to diminish humans to invisibility.

Cheryll and I met Lester at a little Vietnamese restaurant on the edge of Carson City, where, by the time we arrived, he was eating a big bowl of hot-peppered pho and drinking beer. He soon began to reel off amazing stories about his life both before and since coming to Nevada. Lester had been a good suburban kid who, in the mid-1960s, jumped the ship of middle-class respectability to join the freaks in Haight-Ashbury. When the scene in the Haight began to commercialize, he lighted out for the territory, where he became a big-wall climber at Yosemite, routing pitches with rock legends including Galen Rowell, Dick Long, and TM Herbert. Moving from stone to surf, he later lived in Santa Cruz, where he became a skilled sailor. Only after these and other adventures did Lester make his way to the backcountry of Nevada, where he became a world champion in what he calls "dirt boating," a slang term for "land sailing," a challenging sport that, from my point of view, amounts to racing insanely across the playa at speeds of up to 100 miles per hour in a three-wheeled go-cart driven by desert winds that fill a giant sail that rides atop it.

When we asked Lester how he came to acquire Misfits Flat, he said only that he reckoned it would be easier to buy it than to see it posted with No Trespassing signs. No further comment. He had purchased the 2,000-acre tract from the flat's longtime owners, who still had the handwritten receipt showing how much United Artists had paid for the privilege of shooting *The Misfits* there in the summer and fall of 1960. I broke out a printed satellite map of the area, and, over another beer, Lester annotated it for us, indicating various shooting locations. He then gave us directions and permission to spend the afternoon on Misfits Flat.

To get to Lester's desert you roll east from Carson out on "The Loneliest Road in America" (the official designation of US 50), past the Moonlite Bunny Ranch brothel, and, eventually, turn onto the aptly named Breakaheart Road. After bouncing and weaving the truck through potholes, washboard, and frozen mud, we at last came to Lester's gate. After parking the truck there, Cheryll and I hiked through the snow and sage and onto a knoll. From there we had a good view of the expansive playa where the film's indelible mustanging scenes were shot.

Looking out across that snow-dusted alkali flat to the jigsaw-cut mountains beyond, I had an eerie feeling that I had been to this remote place before. And I had, but only because a band of misfit writers and actors were here more than half a century before me. To the west I picked out the pointed peak against which I could picture a particular moment in the film, one in which a roped stallion rears, tethered to and towering over two doomed cowboys who are bracing themselves on their own long shadows. To the east I saw the double-knolled ridge beneath which so much of the picture's final scene was shot—and it had to be shot eastward, because these were afternoon shoots, and they had to be afternoon shoots because the deeply troubled Monroe routinely arrived on the set hours behind schedule. I also made out the gently sweeping desert ridgeline that served as the backdrop for the most dramatic shot in the film: an unforgettable long shot in which the emotionally brittle Roslyn, played by a Monroe who was at least as emotionally brittle as her character, is a tiny speck of dust completely alone out on the playa, shrieking hysterically into space. I re-create the camera position for the shot while Cheryll, in her bright red snowsuit, jogs out onto the snowy playa to the spot where the long dead, eternally youthful Norma Jeane Mortenson once stood, screaming her beautiful blonde head off.

Arthur Miller claimed that we rural Great Basinians are driven into these unpeopled desert expanses by an unnamable and unrequited longing, that we are trying to "escape something somewhere." Maybe this is the same longing that drives a kid from the suburbs to hit the streets of Haight-Ashbury and scale the walls of Yosemite and tack the swells off Santa Cruz and buy his own desert so he will not have to see it posted with No Trespassing signs. Maybe it is the longing that drew me into the beautiful desolation of the western desert, where I can rant in solitude and freedom, screaming my damned head off, like Marilyn Monroe with whiskey and a beard. But if Miller was right that we are the misfits who have washed up on the barren shores of these dry lakes, he missed the most important part of the story, which is that this self-imposed exile is our refuge. To us, these high, dry wilds are home.

Miller and Huston tried to script and shoot the death of the Old West out here on Misfits Flat, but to be in this place is to experience an expansiveness and light that does not give a damn about any of that. Even the poignant loss dramatized in the film is a human-scale emotion that the immensity of the land will not abide. I am reminded of a key moment in *The Misfits*, when Roslyn is asked if she's ever been outside of Reno. "Once I went to the edge of town," she replies. "Doesn't look like there's much out there." To which Gay Langland, the free-spirited old cowboy played so perfectly by Clark Gable, replies with a simple insight that any misfit desert Ranter can understand: "Everything's there."

Bouncing out Breakaheart Road at dusk, we spot six wild horses threading their way slowly through the snowy sage.

I BRAKE FOR RANTS

I HAVE NEVER BEEN A FAN of bumper stickers, though I have always thought the idea had potential. Done properly, you would think a bumper sticker could be a sort of ideological haiku, an elegant little distillation of a person's unique perception of the world; or, alternatively, that it could express genuine wit by being a decent joke that doesn't take too long to tell. And even if a bumper sticker is unlikely to prompt people to act, it should at least make them imagine—as in the classic "Visualize Whirled Peas."

Unfortunately, the problems with bumper stickers outweigh their benefits, and so the immense potential of this unique genre remains unrealized. The first problem with bumper stickers is that they are not site specific. Maybe that is a good thing, if the point of the sticker is to demonstrate your commitment. So if your bumper sticker says "How Can You Be Pro-Life and Eat Dead Animals?" and your car breaks down in front of a cattle ranch, you'll just have to stick to your values during the six days it will take for the local tow-truck driver to agree to help you out. Second, bumper stickers are usually so polemical as to be rhetorically ineffective. Time never moves more slowly than when we are being preached at by somebody's bumper at the First Church of the Red Light.

It is also problematic that so many otherwise promising sticker sound bites are already threadbare and clichéd. It is far too late now to tell folks to "Be the Change You Want to See in the World" (could I somehow *be* colder beer?), "Simplify" (incredibly complicated), or "Love Your Mother" (disturbingly ambiguous). As an environmentalist, I have observed that many "green" bumper stickers are factually incorrect ("Trees Are People Too"), unintentionally ironic ("Question Consumption" on a Lexus), incredibly corny ("May the Forest Be With You"), or intolerably sappy, of which the most egregious is "Keep All of Nature Special!!" This last one manages to be simultaneously saccharine and incomprehensible— never mind that if I used it, I would exhaust my personal annual quota of exclamation points. Finally, environmental stickers rarely respond to issues usefully, because they can't afford to represent more than one point of view. You might see a bumper sticker that says "Save the Earth, Because You Can't Eat Money," but you won't see one that says "You Can't Eat Money, but If You're Starving, You Can Use Money to Buy Food." Once you get away from monolithic ideological pronouncements, bumperfied environmental sloganeering just loses its pop.

I often leave my truck at remote trailheads in the Great Basin, so I have to be mighty careful about what opinions my bumper is blurting out while I am off in the backcountry. It just doesn't pay to stay on your four-wheeled soapbox when you aren't there to defend it. Years ago, I devised a solution that is as ingenious as it is cowardly. I keep a large collection of environmental bumper stickers in a big manila envelope behind the seat of my truck so I can pull out whatever message is called for by the site and occasion. I then temporarily Scotch-Tape the sticker to the inside of the window of the cap on the back of my truck. In this way, I customize my eco-editorializing, depending upon the circumstances and location in which I find myself.

For example, in the parking lot of Reno's Minor League Baseball park, I use "Nature Bats Last," a sticker that has a very different meaning when I use it on spelunking trips. When I go to fetch a case of IPA at our rural liquor store, I put up the perennially popular "Environmental Drinking Team," while at the feed store I use "My Other Car Is a Horse," and at the native-plant nursery I go with the charmingly nerdy "I Brake for Milkweed." At the church rummage sale, I use "Jesus Would Recycle." For the annual fundraising BBQ at our volunteer fire station I break out this incendiary message: "Climate Change Is a Hoax. The Temperature Is Rising Because the Earth Is About to Explode." For use at the university, where bloodless rationality is always at a premium, I actually have a sticker that reads, "The Benefits of Environmental Protection Measures Should Be Thoughtfully Weighed against Their Costs and the Sound Ones Enacted." Professors routinely nod approvingly.

To protect my truck at remote trailheads, I have found that antienvironmental bumper stickers are most effective. I usually go with relatively benign antigreen slogans that offer some sardonic insight ("Keep Environmentalism Pretentious"), or at least some wit ("Vegetarians Taste Better"). As I get farther out into the territory of the Sagebrush Rebels, I am compelled to escalate the rhetoric and shift it rightward. "EPA: Environmental Propaganda Agency" will keep your truck safe almost anywhere in the Great Basin. Also fairly reliable is "My Used Truck Is More Environmentally Responsible than Your New Prius." In fact, any rag on hybrid cars will reduce the chance of a truck break-in by approximately 90 percent. As I reach the remote hinterlands of the desert, extreme measures become necessary. In a few places in central Nevada, I have even posted blatantly irrational messages like "Green Is the New Red. Stop Environmental Communism," though I prefer to stick with absurdity that is leavened by comedy, as in "I'll Start Worrying About Global Warming When I'm Done Bigfoot-Proofing My House." After all, if you are going to adopt an antiscientific worldview that is utterly devoid of logic and rationality, you shouldn't also deprive yourself of humor.

As a result of my spineless, accommodationist bumper-stickering practices, I am well liked everywhere I go, despite the fact that I am a certified curmudgeon. And this, along with not having my tires slashed, seems like a pretty good payoff from a message that costs three bucks and takes three seconds to read. Recently, though, I've decided to take my bumper sticker game up a notch by using my messages not only to affirm bonds with particular audiences but also to get them thinking—if only about bumper stickers. I do this by putting slogans in conversation with one another through the simple but powerful technique of using multiple stickers simultaneously. So, for example, I sometimes display "Global Warming Is Uncool" right next to "Global Warming: The #1 Threat to Unicorns." I especially like to use "I'd Rather Go Naked Than Wear Fur" along with "Save a Tree: Wipe with a Rabbit," since both really help you to visualize their message.

Sometimes my pairings reveal an organizing principle, like the interplanetary focus that emerges when I juxtapose "Earth First: We'll Mine Other Planets Later" with "Keep Earth Clean: It's Not Uranus." I also enjoy the religious theme implied in the simultaneous posting of "Jesus Would Drive a Prius" and "Environmentalism Is Just Another Doomsday Cult." For some perverse reason, I also like using "If You Aren't an Environmentalist You're Suicidal and Should Seek Therapy" next to "World's Sexiest Environmental Psychologist."

You might observe that the "dialogue" my paired bumper stickers provokes is reductive, polemical, and extreme. Fair enough, but I would counter that my dueling messages are about as refined and intelligent as the current state of most environmental discourse, especially in the polarized political landscape of the Intermountain West. My dual pronouncements are not any worse than the toxic language employed by many media outlets, and they may be more nuanced than what we sometimes get from the US Congress. But I do wonder if I should just give up this environmental sloganeering and, since I'm a writer, revert to a single, innocuous bumper sticker that says something like "Supposably Is Still Not a Word," or "Don't Use a Multisyllabic Word Where a Diminutive One Will Suffice," or even "My Life Is Based on a True Story." It might be better, though, just to leave it at this: "I'd Rather Be Ranting."

WILD CHRISTMAS PINYON

BACK IN THE 1970S, when I was a little kid, my family had an artificial Christmas tree that I thought was incredibly cool. It was fun to put together, with a central "trunk" that resembled an oversize broomstick, full of downward-angled holes into which the "branches" were fitted. The "needles" were shiny silver strands of industrial-strength tinsel, and the whole thing was so perfectly symmetrical and so ridiculously garish that it was only a sort of notional Christmas tree, one that was vaguely reminiscent of tree-ness while making no real attempt to resemble anything found in nature. I also talked my mom into buying an electrical device that sat beneath the tree, slowly revolving an illuminated, multicolored wheel, which projected up into the silvery branches light that was by turns yellow, green, blue, and orange. It was the funkiest tree on our street—the disco ball of trees, the kind of Christmas tree Donna Summer or the Bee Gees probably had.

While you might imagine that artificial Christmas trees may be traced back only as far as the glory days of plastic in the 1950s, people actually began making fake holiday trees in the mid-nineteenth century. The practice began in Germany, where extensive deforestation compelled folks to make "trees" out of goose feathers that were dyed green. I don't know what it says about a culture's environmental stewardship when its geese outnumber its trees, but if goose feathers seem like a weird thing to make a tree out of, try optical fiber or holographic Mylar, the latest trends in holiday-spirited arboreal fakery. Eleven million artificial Christmas trees are sold each year, and sales continue to rise in an industry that is worth eight hundred million real dollars annually. And this despite the fact that 80 percent of these fake trees are manufactured in China, where environmentally hazardous lead stabilizer was the chemical du jour in binding the PVC from which the trees are fabricated. Although the recipe has now been changed to tin stabilizer (which somehow doesn't sound much better), the EPA estimates that twenty million artificial Christmas trees still in use in the United States are slowly detonating, toxic lead bombs.

On the other hand, people who buy cut trees shouldn't rush to any sanctimonious claim of superiority over the fake tree people. As it turns out, the farm-raised vs. artificial Christmas tree argument is about on par with paper vs. plastic bags at the grocery checkout. The live tree market is now worth more than a billion bucks annually and employs around a hundred thousand people. But the industry also occupies 350,000 acres of land with a monoculture crop that is not particularly good wildlife habitat and is often treated with pesticides. The spraying, cutting, and transportation of the twenty-five million farm-grown trees sold each year also generates almost two billion pounds of greenhouse gases. I get it that nobody wants to decorate their Christmas tree while pondering its contribution to global climate change, and I'm also aware that the acres not given to Christmas tree production are more likely to be planted in fertilizer-soaked GMO corn than protected as sanctuaries of wildness and biodiversity. Still, I don't want you live tree folks to jump to the conclusion that you're necessarily more righteous than your neighbors just because your tree arrived in an eighteen-wheeler instead of a cardboard box.

But the fake vs. farm-raised fork in Christmas Tree Road (which reminds me of Yogi Berra's sage advice that "when you come to a fork in the road, take it!") leaves out a third route—a practice that was once ubiquitous but is now so statistically insignificant that the Christmas tree data nerds don't even bother counting it: hoofing out into the wilds to cut your own tree. Our annual family tradition is to take Hannah and Caroline, join the family of our buddies Cheryll and Steve, and head out into the wilderness of central Nevada to cut our Christmas tree. You might think the Great Basin Desert, which is a vast sagebrush ocean dotted by glaring, white islands of salt-encrusted alkali flats, would be an uninviting place to hunt up a decent tree. Not so. Nevada, the most mountainous state in the lower forty-eight, has more than three hundred mountain ranges, most of which are home to "the PJs": desert rat shorthand for a high-elevation desert forest consisting of dominant pinyon pine–juniper woodland.

In our part of this big desert, the pinyon-juniper biome occurs above about 4,000 feet and below the alpine zone. It requires ten to twenty inches of annual precipitation (which falls mostly as snow), and so it exists in a band above the lower-elevation sagebrush steppe, which receives only four to eight inches of moisture. Although the PJs contain some scattered sage, rabbitbrush, and ephedra—even an occasional Jeffrey pine—this environment consists almost exclusively of pinyon pine and juniper trees. While many people picture our part of the West as a bleak, treeless desert, almost twenty million acres of the Great Basin (nearly a fifth of its total land area) is occupied by the PJs.

In fact, these pinyon pine–juniper forests are colonizing more ground every year. Since the mid-nineteenth century, the PJs have expanded at least threefold, and perhaps as much as tenfold. This expansion and infill, which has been caused by a number of factors, including overgrazing and fire exclusion, is now encroaching on the sagebrush ecosystems that are home to threatened species such as the pygmy rabbit and greater sage grouse. Land managers here in the Great Basin are using fire—and fire surrogates like thinning—to check the expansion of the PJs and protect the sagebrush biome they are successfully invading from above.

Our annual pilgrimage to find a wild Christmas tree takes us to almost 7,500 feet in the Desatoya Range, on BLM lands about 135 miles east of Ranting Hill. There we hike, search for fossils, play with the dogs, and scrape away enough snow to build a bonfire of dead sage, around which we gather to swap family stories, eat snacks, and drink warm "Abuelita" cocoa and chilled rye whiskey. The tree cutting is only a small part of a long, lovely day in the snowy, high desert mountains. Our BLM Christmas tree tag costs a whopping five bucks—about a tenth the average cost of a farm-raised, commercially sold tree—and while we burn plenty of gas in our pickup to get our tree, we'd be headed into the hinterlands to hike and snowshoe whether we were tree hunting or not.

While slaying a wild tree for one's own ritual purposes might appear environmentally destructive, by cutting in BLM-identified areas we're functioning as members of a volunteer crew of stand thinners who work to reduce fire danger and stem the advance of the PJs on the fragile sagebrush biome below. I realize that this claim may sound suspiciously virtuous. The plain truth is that we love to be in the mountains in winter, sharing a family outing in a remote, spectacularly beautiful part of our home desert. If circumstances were reversed, and a farm-raised tree cost five bucks while the BLM tree tag cost fifty, we'd still be driving past the commercial tree lots in town on our way out to the desert to find a pinyon pine for our family's holiday tree.

The species of pine we cut is single-leaf pinyon (*Pinus monophylla*), the state tree of Nevada, although in the interest of full disclosure I should note that we have two state trees; the other is the bristlecone pine, which can reach ages upward of four thousand years. (The only other state to have two state trees is neighboring California, with whom we compete at every opportunity.) *Pinus monophylla* is a beautiful high desert tree: short-needled, gray-green, thirty or forty feet in height and about as wide as it is tall, gnarled, twisting, and wildly branching when mature, but when young, handsomely columnar.

This tree is remarkable in many ways. For starters, it is the only single-needled pine on the planet (note to the 99 percent of us who routinely use the word "unique" incorrectly: perfectly fine to employ it here). It is also the most xeric pine in North America, enduring conditions of aridity and temperature extremes almost beyond imagination. And it is an old-time Westerner. Fossil pollen records and fossil needles in ancient packrat middens show that the pinyon pine, having moseyed north to the Great Basin after the last ice age, has been native here for thousands of years. Individual trees can reach ages of more than nine hundred years and usually don't become very productive of cones until they've been standing around for a half century or so.

The seeds hidden within those cones are the pinyon's most extraordinary feature. While all pines produce edible seeds, the pinyon's seed is so unusually large as to be a major food source for both humans and many species of rodents and birds—including the pinyon jay (*Gymnorhinus cyanocephalus*), whose harvesting and caching of the tree's seeds is an important mechanism of its dispersal. Pinyon nuts not only are large and delicious but also have exceptional nutritional value. They are high in iron, manganese, and other essential minerals, are loaded with vitamins A and E, riboflavin, niacin, and antioxidants, and contain all twenty of the amino acids. They are even gluten-free. And, at 3,000 calories per pound, pine nuts boast a fat content exceeding that of chocolate—thus providing a nutritional density that has made them a highly valued wild food. Although the pinyon was not scientifically described until the mid-nineteenth century, the wonders of its delicious, nutritious nut have been known to Europeans since the tree's use by Indian peoples was first reported by Spanish explorer Cabeza de Vaca in 1535.

Pinyon nuts have played a vital role in Native American cultures, and evidence suggests that this food source was important to the prehistoric peoples of the Great Basin, just as it is still culturally important to our Northern Paiute and Western Shoshone neighbors. Long before the appearance of the Christ who is celebrated with the Christmas tree, the native peoples of these high, cold deserts made posts from the bole of the pinyon tree, and enjoyed the special aroma of this pine as its branches crackled in an open fire that provided welcome warmth. Pinyon pitch forms an adhesive so powerful that it was used to mend cracked water jars, and, in its boiled form, was employed as a waterproofing that was applied to basketry and to the cradle boards in which infants were carried from one pinyon grove to another. Medicinally, pinyon resin was placed on a rabbit fur patch that was applied to wounds as an antiseptic, while the needles were boiled into teas and ground into powders that were used to remedy a range of maladies. Pine nuts were gathered, processed, stored, and consumed in an impressive variety of ingenious ways, while their harvest each fall was a major ceremonial and community event—just as it still is today. It has been said that the pine nut was as important to the native inhabitants of the Great Basin as the bison was to the plains peoples.

In *Walden* (1854), which was published at exactly the historical moment when Christmas trees first became commercially available in America, Henry Thoreau wrote that "it is a vulgar error to suppose that you have tasted huckleberries who never plucked them." "A huckleberry never reaches Boston," he concluded, because "the ambrosial and essential part of the fruit is lost with the bloom which is rubbed off in the market cart, and they become mere provender." Thoreau here makes two points that are repeated throughout his work: the first is that the sweetness of nature's fruit is produced as much by our experience of nature as by the taste of the fruit itself; the second is that commodification of nature tends to compromise its meaning and significance.

Like Thoreau's wild huckleberry, our pinyon pine Christmas tree is something we harvested ourselves from the wilderness, and that is one of the many reasons we find it so beautiful. And with it we have harvested a memorable shared experience. When we gather by the woodstove to admire this pinyon shining in our home here on Ranting Hill, we see not just a Christmas tree but also windswept high-elevation ridges and canyons, the rippling texture of bleached vermillion cliffs, the crests of range after snowy range flowing out to the distant horizon. We hear the sweep of downcanyon wind and the croak of jet-black ravens and the crackle of a little bonfire, smell pinyon pitch and hot cocoa, whiskey and sage. We remember tromping through the snow, as a family, deciding together that *this* is the wild tree we will bring home and decorate, and beneath whose boughs we will place our gifts.

Our Christmas tree is neither as green nor as shapely as a farm-raised tree. It grew more than 100 miles away from our home hill and so will never be as handy by as would an artificial tree. It is almost too heavy to carry, too brushy to decorate, and too pitchy to handle. Its short, stiff, sharp, single needles jab us as we coast by it with warm milk or chilled eggnog in hand. As a Christmas tree, our pinyon pine could not possibly be more inconvenient. And that is yet one more way of saying that, to us, it is perfect.

AN ASSAY ON
AULD LANG SYNE

Every New Year's Eve, drunk people from around the world sing some approximation of "Auld Lang Syne," a song whose words they rarely know—though one of the song's many virtues is that, when arm-in-arm revelers slur out "For hold and sign" or "Four old aunts shine" or "Fart old Ann Zyne," it still sounds damned good. But even when we do know the words, we do not know what they mean. This confusion is forgivable, since in the Scots language "Auld Lang Syne" literally means "old long since" (huh?), and even idiomatic translations like "days gone by" or "long long ago" do not entirely clarify the term. As Billy Crystal's character puts it in the 1989 chick flick *When Harry Met Sally*, "'should old acquaintance be forgot?' Does that mean that we should forget old acquaintances? Or does it mean that if we happened to forget them, we should remember them, which is not possible, because we already forgot them?"

"Auld Lang Syne" emerged from the great Lowland Scots ballad tradition but is most closely associated with Robert Burns, who recrafted the song as a beautiful poem that was published in 1788. As Scots, including my own kin, emigrated to every corner of the globe, they took this traditional ballad with them. It thus became Scotland's greatest cultural export—though, in fairness, the competition was haggis, bagpipes, and plaid skirts for men—and is now beloved by inebriated folks the world over. The version of Burns's poem we sing today is radically simplified and omits a number of lovely verses that, if sung in the original Scots, would make a challenging field sobriety test. My favorite of these is Bobby's original closing verse:

> And there's a hand, my trusty fiere!
> And gie's a hand o' thine.
> And we'll tak a right gude-willie-waught,
> For auld lang syne.

On the off chance you're as confused as the characters in *When Harry Met Sally*, "willie waught" is the world's most lyrical euphemism for drink. Here, then, is Burns's poetic celebration of hand clasping and cup raising in memory of times gone by. It is among the oldest, most meaningful gestures known to human culture.

Thinking about this song caused me to wonder if anything in Nevada might be named for it, which eventually led me to Auld Lang Syne Peak, an obscure, 7,400-foot mountain out in the north-central part of the state. I say "obscure" because this mountain abides in a nearly uninhabited stretch of the Great Basin, where it stands amid innumerable other mountains, including much higher ones like Star Peak and Thunder Mountain, nearly 10,000-footers in the nearby Humboldt Range, where Mark Twain went broke chasing silver during the early 1860s. But it was the name of the peak that drew me, not its lofty elevation, and so I called my hiking buddies Cheryll and Steve to invite them to join me in exploring

Auld Lang Syne Peak the following day, December 31. I hoped that this dry winter might make the peak accessible, though in many years it would not be a feasible climb at this time of year.

My friends did not hesitate when I called, and so the next morning found us on the road, speeding east into the open heart of the Great Basin. A two-hour drive from our homes took us from Northern Paiute country out into Western Shoshone country, and eventually we pulled off to recaffeinate at Puckerbrush, Nevada, where a dilapidated sign informed us that we were at 4,288 feet in a town whose population stands at twenty-eight. But no town was in evidence, just a truck stop with road food, strong coffee, pints of liquor, and those kitschy, rear-view mirror dream catchers, which comprise four of the five things a long-haul trucker needs (the fifth is available at the PussyCat, down the highway a stretch toward Winnemucca). From Puckerbrush we rattled overland on washboarded BLM roads through open-range ranching country, then past a small, placer gold-mining operation. I glimpsed the feed hopper and rotating grizzly as we wound through the site, past the settling pond, and then upcanyon into the historic Dun Glen mining area, where we parked the truck off in the sage and clambered out to gear up for our hike.

Founded in 1862, Dun Glen boomed for thirty years before simply vanishing in the early 1890s. All that remains of the miners who sought their wild fortune here are a few broken-down remains of cabins that were hand-dug into a hillside above Dun Glen Creek. We explore these remnant structures, admiring the construction of their hand-laid stone foundations, wondering what it might have been like to eke out a life in this remote place one hundred fifty years ago. I notice the fractured, bone-colored loop of a teacup's handle, set carefully on a foundation rock—a reminder that families lived here. Perhaps some, like my own, were brightened by two beautiful little girls, growing up too quickly.

A mile or so into the hike we ascend a low ridge from which the peak comes into view. It is an anticlimactic moment, as the mountain appears to be an unimpressive dome, barely worthy of a stroll, let alone a 300-mile round-trip. I apologize to Cheryll and Steve for dragging them all the way out here for what looks like a mild constitutional.

"Let's find something else to climb while we're here, y'all, 'cause in short order Auld Lang Syne will be in our past," I say.

"We'll see," Steve replies. "There's more vertical out here than you'd think."

Our route is up the low ridge, then across the canyon mouth via what looks like an earthen dam but is actually a giant pile of mine tailings. We scramble up a steep, rocky slope, where the detritus of old mining operations is everywhere visible. Here are the collapsed remnants of a tin shed, there a prospect hole transformed into a mirror by snowmelt. We guess at the vintage of what we find by observing the nature of the junk. Cheryll finds a piece of threaded pipe, which became widely available in the 1880s. Steve notices a few nails with round rather than square heads, an innovation that dates to the invention of wire nails in the early 1890s. We also find shards of old bottles, many of which are sun purpled, an effect produced when the magnesium dioxide–infused clear glass produced during the second half of the nineteenth century is transformed into a lovely hue of lavender by long exposure to the sun's ultraviolet rays. Here, on this remote desert mountain, we are surrounded by the scattered fragments of auld lang syne.

Even on the steepest pitches we find vertical shafts whose bottoms remain invisible, though the echoes that return when we drop a chunk of rose quartz into one suggest impressive depth. Soon, we stumble upon an actual mine shaft, which we peek into but know better than to enter. It is difficult to picture people up here so long ago, ghosts digging into the earth with their hands. I wonder if they found what they were looking for inside this dark hole, on the flank of this mountain, in the middle of this isolated, illimitable expanse of desert. It is the kind of place where it is possible to imagine great dreams being fulfilled, but much easier to imagine them perishing forever.

Climbing above the long-abandoned mine, we begin what turns out to be a surprisingly difficult ascent through the scree, as we separate and traverse obliquely across the north face of a high ridge and toward a narrow saddle that is slung below the peak. Keeping my head down as I cross the steep slope, I see plenty of scat. Probably elk, since it appears large, roundish-oval, and less dimpled than mule deer scat tends to be, though this rough terrain and high elevation also make desert bighorn sheep a possibility. As I pick my way across the steep face, I occasionally go to a three-point scramble, using my uphill hand to stabilize my footing and work my way toward the still-distant peak. It is on this slippery traverse that my faulty estimation of the wee climb becomes palpable, and I suck wind working to achieve the saddle, which appears to recede before me. Pausing to catch my breath, I lift my head to discover that a second mountain has come into view. Behind what I assumed was Auld Lang Syne is a sister peak that is more distant and also higher. It is, in fact, this more distant of the twin summits that we are bound for, and while we are already several hours into this climb, it is apparent there are more hours ahead.

Having tackled the long traverse by our independent routes, Steve and Cheryll and I meet up at a rock outcropping on the saddle below the sister summits. I am the last to arrive. We break here for water and trail food and to absorb the expansive view. While leaning back against a boulder, I notice a golden eagle describing perfect circles directly over the crown of What Used to Be Auld Lang Syne Peak, as if signaling that this unnamed summit may yet hold some special significance.

"That's so beautiful," Cheryll remarks, admiring the eagle's effortless gyre. "Perfect! You should write about *that.*"

"A lone eagle, ignited by shattered sunlight, describing perfect circles over the crown of a domed peak, as if signaling that this unnamed summit may yet hold some special significance?" I reply. "I can't write about that. Way too nature-writery. Sounds staged. *We* know this is actually happening, but readers will think it's horseshit." Smiling, Steve points silently to a nearby pile of wild mustang dung.

"Well played," I reply in response to his wordless punch line. The eagle circles a few more times, counterclockwise, winding the hands of time backward, and then is gone.

Now, for the final pitch of the climb. We scramble around the shoulder of What Used to Be Auld Lang Syne Peak onto a rocky bridge between the twin summits and then start straight up the exposed crown of the mountain. This is the most difficult part of the climb but also the shortest, and we soon find ourselves standing together atop the peak. Once again, I am the last to arrive, and Cheryll greets me with a serenade that she has secretly arranged in order to celebrate the occasion. She has loaded a melancholy pop version of "Auld Lang Syne" onto her phone, from which she now plays a crooning, heartbreaking take on Bobby Burns's timeless gem.

The moment is intended to be ironic: we three outdoor enthusiasts self-consciously reveling in the summit climax of a wilderness experience by cranking sappy tunes on a smartphone. But the genius of this song is that it will brook no irony. While I acknowledge the wisdom of the maxim that "nostalgia ain't what it used to be," the Burns ballad belies any hip dismissal of the imaginative power the past wields over our experience of the present. This song is the world's greatest anthem to ephemerality, a poignant expression of the impossible desire to check the rush of time, to turn back on the trail, if only for a moment, toward the always already-lost country of our past. Soon, we will begin our descent, put the mountain behind us, perhaps even reach home before the old year turns to the new. For the moment, though, there is only the stopped time of this summit, and the bittersweet notes of a song that refuses to let us forget the past.

As I listen to the song's verse about friends separated by oceans, and by oceans of time, I think of the families who lived here one hundred fifty years ago. When the Dun Glen miners scoured these hills, they had to assay what they dug out of the earth. *Assay*, which in its mining context refers to the testing of ore to determine its quality, is actually a much older word and one with broader connotations. Since the fourteenth century, an *assay* has been a "trial, test of quality, test of character." To assay is to "try, endeavor, strive." The sister word to *assay* is *essay*, whose etymological origins also point to the idea of trying, and of trial. An essay is a weighing, an examination, an endeavor. An essay, ever and always, is an attempt.

As the would-be irony of the song is overwhelmed by the genuine emotion it inspires, I assay in all directions from the summit of Auld Lang Syne. It is wide-open country as far as I am able to see, with alkali and sage playas rolled out gracefully between endless folds of white-capped mountains, ranges receding one behind the other into this boundless ocean of high desert. In one direction a lowering storm settles on a darkening range with veiled fingers of virga, the vanishing rain that evaporates before it reaches the earth; in the other direction is a basin dramatically illuminated by the late-afternoon sun as it descends through azure notches in an unbroken mat of silver, flat-bottomed clouds. Which is the view of the past, I wonder, and which the future? Time will tell. Until it does, we'll take a cup o' kindness yet, for auld lang syne.

THE BUCKET LIST

A STUDY PUBLISHED in a respectable journal of psychiatry was resurrected in the tabloids after it suggested that successful comedians often show characteristics typically found in folks suffering from schizophrenia and bipolar disorder. A scientifically demonstrable link between humor and insanity had momentarily captured the feeble imagination of a public that likes to think of comedy as a form of divine madness and so had rushed to embrace the dubious proposition that the wise fools who produce it are necessarily both gifted and troubled. Apparently, this is not the same public that attends Hollywood film comedies, which consist primarily of fart jokes aimed at a core demographic of fourteen-year-old boys. So poor is the comic fare at the Cineplex (which itself sounds like the name of a sexually transmitted disease) that even I, an aficionado of flatulence humor, have thrown in the towel. We have simply come too far from the quality fart jokes of Shakespeare. (In *Othello*, the musician asks the clown, "Whereby hangs a tail, sir?" To which the clown replies, "By many a wind instrument that I know.")

In response to the immoderate public enthusiasm for this study, comedienne Sara Pascoe wrote a brilliant reply, in which she flatly points out that being a humorist is a job, and that some people succeed at it because they work hard. Comedy, she observes, is a craft, a practice, a skill, and, often, a grind. (Here, I am reminded of Twain, who complained in a letter that "for *seven weeks* I have not had my natural rest but have been a night-and-day sick-nurse to my wife . . . and yet must turn in now and write a damned *humorous* article.") Well, this "craft and grind" explanation of humor offered a disappointingly unheroic gloss, what with its total absence of insanity and genius. After all, who wants to be told that something that makes them laugh actually took a long time to create and was terribly hard work? If people prefer to see industrious, workmanlike humorists as insane geniuses, I don't see a decent reason to mess that up. Always better to be funny than right.

One of Pascoe's observations, however, caught my attention. Commenting that the creativity of the humorist "allows a much more childlike approach to life," she goes on to say that if the researchers had administered their test to 523 children instead of to 523 professional comedians (where did they find so many?), the kids would "all be hugely 'psychotic' in their thinking." As a parent, I found this assertion that children are universally insane more interesting and more accurate than the claim that humor is fatally correlated with adult psychopathology.

I had a chance to test this proposition on New Year's Day, when Hannah and Caroline decided that everyone in our family should look to the future by producing a bucket list. I had long intended to draft a bucket list, but had been kept from it by the obvious impediment that thinking about what you want to do before you die means thinking about dying, which is even less entertaining than a Hollywood fart joke. Eryn claims that I have "mortality issues," which is accurate only if preferring life to death constitutes an "issue." I am from the Woody Allen school on this one: "I don't want to achieve immortality through my work," wrote Allen, "I want to achieve immortality through not dying." Still, it wasn't easy to say no to the girls, and so we all agreed to work on our personal bucket lists.

Hannah and Caroline had so much fun with their project that by the end of New Year's Day, they had already posted their two lists—with a combined total of more than one hundred fifty entries—on the outside of their bedroom door. In this same time, I had constructed a bucket list that consisted, literally, of a single entry: "Make a bucket list." In fairness, I am not a very expeditious list-maker, even when the topic is more pleasant than "Stuff I want to get done before I die." After all, it took me two decades to complete my "List of Things That Actually Work," which to this day includes only WD-40, bourbon, and *Moby-Dick*. Still, the girls had good cause to complain that I did not seem to be working very hard on my list. Their lists were not only completed (and decorated!) but publicly posted, like Martin Luther's theses on the church door, while I had only my one, pathetic little entry. It didn't help that my list, such as it was, was scribbled in shop pencil on the back of an old liquor store receipt.

Needing to divert the focus from my own failure, I decided to take a close look at the girls' bucket lists. After all, how could they have produced anything decent in such a short time? As I read through their lists, though, I was impressed not only by the range and creativity of what Hannah and Caroline had come up with, but also by their uninhibited spontaneity and originality. The lists did look as if they had been made by insane people—but by imaginative, caring, insane people who recognize no limits to what is possible.

I examined Hannah's list first. It contained a lot of adventures I wish I had thought to put on my own list, including "hang glide," "make an album of my own cool music," "play basketball in the snow," and "be an extra in a movie." But along with these proposed escapades were some items whose beauty was in their everyday nature: "fill a jar with buttons," "babysit for somebody other than my sister," "go a week without making my bed," "finish a book in a day." There was also a good bit more philanthropy than my own unwritten list would have contained. Hannah wanted to "feed homeless people," "read stories at a senior home," and "help poor children," all of which made my own life's goals—which, if I could ever articulate them, would include "drink better rye," "cuss out my boss," and "heckle more at baseball games"—seem selfish and ill-conceived. Hannah's list showed a desire to travel, and, while she included visits to Canada, London, and New Orleans, she also listed "ride my bike in California," which was not very exotic, given our close proximity to the Golden State.

I also noticed that Hannah's list contained items that were easy as pie right along with those that were pie in the sky. For example, "participate in a pie-eating contest" appeared just a few entries away from "become a famous inventor." "Build a big snowman" was right next to "meet the president." And the desert figured prominently in Hannah's list. "Own a rattlesnake," "hike up the canyon to watch the moon rise," and "sing a concert for the coyotes" were among the things she hopes to accomplish. Hannah's bucket list also expressed an urge to delight others. She wanted to "count how many people I can make smile" and "get a whole room of people laughing."

Little Caroline's list was, if anything, even more interesting. Like her big sister's bucket list, Caroline's oscillated wildly from the mundane to the fantastic. "Get a white cat" was number 42 on her list; number 43 was "be an astronaut." "Dye rocks" was immediately next to "climb the Eiffel Tower with ropes," and "have a pet hamster" was adjacent to "ride a shark" (there was a lot of animal riding on her list: shark, seal, jaguar, kangaroo, and giraffe).

"Work at a pool" was immediately preceded by "touch the moon." "Eat cake with my hands" was not far from "carve a giant totem pole." Also like Hannah, little sister had constructed a list that revealed an earnest philanthropic sentiment. While Caroline aspired to "own a hundred-year-old mansion," she also wanted to "own an orphanage and give kids ice cream every day." And, in addition to planning to "give flowers to a stranger," she expressed the generous but disturbing ambition to "have a big sleepover with random people off the street."

Given Caroline's personality, I should have guessed that she wants to "climb a volcano," "make a world record," and "form a band called the 'Fire Breathing Unicorns.'" But she also has some simple dreams: to "use a walkie-talkie," "have a tug-o-war over a mud pit," and "dance in the rain." Also like her sister, many of Caroline's life goals arise from her home desert. She wants to "pan for gold," "find the end of a desert rainbow," and, for some reason, "eat a kangaroo rat." She also plans to "mountain bike across Spain, Thailand, and Massachusetts." My favorite entry on her list was "dream about visiting a beautiful island." When I asked Caroline why she thought it would be so wonderful to visit an island, she corrected me, emphatically: "No, Dad, *dream about* visiting an island!"

No grown-up I know would make a to-do list including something they ought to dream about doing. Hell, we wouldn't even add to our bucket list that we want to touch the moon—though of course we do—because we'd shoot the rocket of that fantasy down before it could lift off our cognitive launchpad. (If Neil Armstrong had a bucket list when he was five years old, I hope it included "touch the moon.") I am unsure we'd even admit to ourselves that we'd like to carve a totem pole or dance in the rain or eat cake with our hands. Maybe that is why I couldn't make a decent bucket list: because as a grown-up I've fallen into the dark habit of editing life's possibilities before they can be written, perhaps even before they can be thought. This represents not only a terrible failure of imagination but an active repression of it. I had only one thing on my bucket list—to make a bucket list—and I still could not get it done. Reflecting on fame, legendary southpaw rock guitarist Jimi Hendrix once observed, "Once you are dead, you are made for life." Well, he ought to know. But for those of us who have not kicked the bucket yet, success remains less certain. Should I try for world peace right away, or start with hang gliding and work my way up? If every moment is unutterably precious, which it so clearly is, where then should we begin the race to fulfill our dreams while there is still time left to try?

Within a few days of creating their wonderful bucket lists, the girls did something else that most grown-ups would find challenging: they set out to actually do as many of the listed activities as possible, placing a check mark next to each as it was completed. Hannah was able to "read a book in one day" and "make a parody of a song," while Caroline managed to "dye rocks" and, thanks to the remoteness of Ranting Hill, "snort at an antelope." A freak desert downpour made it possible for both kids to "dance in the rain."

Hoping to get into the spirit of their attempt to accomplish the things on their bucket lists, I scanned the lists for something more immediately achievable than "touch the moon." When I did, I saw an item on Caroline's list that I had not noticed before: "paint me and Hannah on a wall."

"What do you mean by this one?" I asked Caroline, pointing to number 37 on her list.

"You know, me and Hannah stand against a wall, like we're shadows, and then we paint the shapes of our shadows on the wall," she explained, with obvious concern that I might be too dim-witted to grasp the concept.

The Bucket List / 201

"OK, I get it now. You and sister grab some play chalk and come with me," I instructed, heading out the door. The girls soon followed me out to the toolshed, where I had found the better part of a gallon of cherry-apple red paint and a pair of old brushes. "Now, y'all stand against the shed in any position you want."

"Really? This is going to be *epic!*" exlaimed Caroline. Hannah announced, excitedly, that she intended to put this painting thing on her bucket list too so she could check it off later. The girls took their positions against the shed, remaining frozen, while I patiently chalked their "shadows" against the tan wall of the out-building. Hannah posed with her arms up, in the biceps flex of a bodybuilder; little Caroline struck the pose of a superhero about to take flight. I popped the paint can open with my pocketknife, handed each of our girls a brush, and suggested that they get to work on their bucket list.

Eryn and I sat nearby on a pair of bucked juniper logs and watched Hannah Virginia and Caroline Emerson at play. It took them a good while, but they never tired of the project, which they laughed their way through. Although Caroline accidentally painted Beauregard, the dog, a little, things went pretty smoothly. When the final strokes were complete, we all stood back to admire what had been wrought. The girls' bright-red silhouettes jumped off the drab wall of the shed, and two cherry-apple shadows of joy were added to our high desert fauna. In that moment, as we gathered to congratulate the girls on their painting, I finally realized exactly where to begin work on my own bucket list: anywhere.

That evening we had a fine supper together. Afterward, we all ate cake with our hands.

CREDITS

The "Rants from the Hill" essay series that eventually led to this book was published in *High Country News*, where the Rants ran online every month from July 2010 through April 2016.

In addition, the following Rants were published in the print edition of *High Country News*:

"Balloons on the Moon." *High Country News* 44.13 (August 6, 2012): 22.

"In Defense of Bibliopedestrianism." *High Country News* 45.21 (December 9, 2013): 26.

"Hunting for Scorpions." *High Country News* 46.22 (December 22, 2014): endpaper.

A number of Rants were reprinted in other venues, as follows:

"After Ten Thousand Years." *Libertas* 3 (April 2009): 6–7.

"All I Need for a Walk Is a Good Book." [Revised version of "In Defense of Bibliopedestrianism."] *Reader's Digest* 183.1100 (June 2014): 100–103.

"Customer Cranky" and "Lucy the Desert Cat" appeared as part of "Excerpts from *Rants from the Hill.*" *The Nevada Review* 4.3 (Fall 2012): 83–96.

"Guests in the House of Fire" appeared as part of "Excerpts from *Rants from the Hill.*" *The Nevada Review* 5.1 (Spring 2013): 24–28.

"Scaling Piedmonts." [Contains passages from "After Ten Thousand Years."] *Hobart Park* (2009): 111–19.

ACKNOWLEDGMENTS

WRITERS ARE VERY MUCH IN NEED of friends, and I have been fortunate to have so many in my life and in my corner. Here I offer my sincere thanks, along with equally sincere apologies to anyone I may have neglected to include.

Among fellow writers of environmental creative nonfiction, my thanks go to Rick Bass, Paul Bogard, John Calderazzo, SueEllen Campbell, Laird Christensen, Casey Clabough, Jennifer Cognard-Black, Chris Cokinos, John Elder, Andy Furman, Dimitri Keriotis, Ian Marshall, Kate Miles, Kathy Moore, John Murray, Nick Neely, Sean O'Grady, Tim Palmer, Bob Pyle, David Quammen, Eve Quesnel, Janisse Ray, Suzanne Roberts, Chris Robertson, Leslie Ryan, Terre Ryan, Gary Snyder, John Tallmadge, David Taylor, and Rick Van Noy. Very special thanks to David Gessner, John Lane, and John Price, whose support has been decisive.

Thanks also for the encouragement I've received from other friends in the environmental literature and humor studies communities, including Tom Bailey, Patrick Barron, Jim Bishop, Kate Chandler, Ben Click, Tammy Cloutier, Nancy Cook, Jerry Dollar, Ann Fisher-Wirth, Tom Hillard, Heather Houser, Richard Hunt, Dave Johnson, Rochelle Johnson, Mark Long, Tom Lynch, Kyhl Lyndgaard, Annie Merrill, Clint Mohs, David Morris, Dan Philippon, Justin Race, Steve Railton, Heidi Scott, Robert Sickels, Dave Stentiford, Jim Warren, Alan Weltzein, and Tracy Wuster.

Closer to home, I'd like to offer thanks to fellow Great Basin writers Bill Fox, Shaun Griffin, Ann Ronald, Rebecca Solnit, Steve

Trimble, Claire Watkins, and Terry Tempest Williams, with a nod to the desert writers who led the way: Mary Austin, Ed Abbey, Ellen Meloy, and Chuck Bowden. Thanks to my colleagues in the MFA program at the University of Nevada, Reno: Steve Gehrke, Sarah Hulse, Ann Keniston, Gailmarie Pahmeier, and, especially, Chris Coake. And thanks to my students in the courses on American humor writing, place-based creative nonfiction, and western American literary nonfiction that I taught during 2014, 2015, and 2016.

Among Reno friends, I've received valuable support from Pete Barbieri, Mike Colpo, Fil Corbitt, Donnie Curtis, Dondo Darue, David Fenimore, Daniel Fergus, Mark Gandolfo, Betty Glass, Torben Hansen, Aaron and Diana Hiibel, Kent Irwin, Rich Kentz, Jo Landis, Tony Marek, Ashley Marshall, Katie O'Connor, Eric Rasmussen, Erin Read, Meri Shadley, and Jacque Sundstrand. Timely, professional editorial assistance from Laura Ofstad was crucial in bringing this book into port. And special thanks to my closest friends, Colin and Monica Robertson and Cheryll and Steve Glotfelty. The most significant support I have received outside my family came from Cheryll, whose encouragement has been essential to my growth as a writer.

I've been fortunate to benefit from productive collaborations with many talented and industrious editors. Following are a few of these folks, along with the magazine or press at which they worked at the time I received their help. Chip Blake, Jennifer Sahn, Hannah Fries, Kristen Hewitt, and Taylor Brorby (*Orion*); David Gessner, Ben George, and Anna Lena Phillips (*Ecotone*); Kate Miles (*Hawk & Handsaw*); Chris Cokinos (*Isotope*); Nick Neely (*Watershed*); Rowland Russell (*Whole Terrain*); Nancy Levinson (*Places Journal*); Jamie Iredell (*New South*); Mike Colpo (Patagonia's *The Cleanest Line*); Tara Zades (*Reader's Digest*); Justin Raymond (*Shavings*); Jeanie French (*Red Rock Review*); Bruce Anderson (*Sunset*); Caleb Cage and Joe McCoy (*The Nevada Review*); Fil Corbitt (*Van

Sounds); Jason Leppig (*Island Press Field Notes*); Brad Rassler (*Sustainable Play*); Barry Tharaud (*Nineteenth-Century Prose*); Greg Garrard (Oxford University Press); Jonathan Cobb (Island Press); and Boyd Zenner (University of Virginia Press). Thanks also to Jessica Ziegler, of Vestor Logic, who constructed my website; it can be found at http://michaelbranchwriter.com/.

My sincere thanks go to the many generous and hardworking folks at *High Country News*, where the "Rants from the Hill" essay series that led to this book ran online each month from July 2010 through April 2016. My friend and former student Nick Neely suggested me to *High Country News* while he was working with the magazine as an intern, which put the series in motion. The support and assistance of editors Stephanie Paige Ogburn, Jodi Peterson, Paul Larmer, Tay Wiles, Michelle Nijhuis, Diane Sylvain, Cally Carswell, Emily Guerin, and Kate Schimel made it possible for a diverse and enthusiastic readership to spend a few minutes each month with my unusual way of seeing the world. This book would not have been possible without the support of the amazing community of editors, writers, scientists, readers, and activists that has formed around the vitally important work accomplished by *High Country News*.

I'd also like to express my appreciation for the many teachers and readers who have shared these essays. Pieces included in this book have been taught in creative writing or environmental literature courses in at least twenty-five states and have received more than a hundred thousand page views online. Of course a kitten video posted to YouTube receives more hits than this in an hour, so I'm certainly not bragging, but it's gratifying to know that so many readers have enjoyed sharing glimpses of our dry slice of life in the high desert.

I want to offer very special thanks to George F. Thompson of GFT Publishing. It is impossible to imagine the current vitality of the environmental humanities without the quality books George has brought into the world over the past three decades. I first began collaborating with George in 1992, when my friend Dan Philippon and I pitched him a book on nature writing from Virginia's Blue Ridge Mountains and Shenandoah Valley. Although Dan and I were still in graduate school at the time, George took a chance on us, and *The Height of Our Mountains* (Johns Hopkins University Press, 1998) became part of George's legendary Center for American Places publishing program. Now, a quarter century later, George's insightful feedback on an earlier version of this manuscript was crucial in helping to shape it for publication.

I want to express my sincere gratitude to the terrific team at Shambhala/Roost Books, whose work on my 2016 book, *Raising Wild: Dispatches from a Home in the Wilderness*, convinced me that I had found a home with them. Thanks to Julia Gaviria (assistant editor) for seeing the manuscript down the final stretch, and to Daniel Urban-Brown (art director) for making it a thing of beauty. And thanks to the inimitable KJ Grow (sales and marketing manager), Claire Kelly (senior marketing manager), and Jess Townsend (publicist), whose excellent work has helped this book to find its readers. Most important, I offer my deepest and most sincere thanks to Jennifer Urban-Brown (editor). My ongoing collaboration with Jenn continues to be among the most productive and enjoyable of my career, and I can only hope that folks who believe that a writer's relationship with their editor must be adversarial might be as fortunate as I have been in having such a supportive, patient, insightful collaborator in their work.

I am blessed with a family that is exceptionally tolerant of my eccentricities and ambitions, my fierce sense of place and idiosyncratic sense of humor. On the other side of the Sierra, thanks to our Central Valley people: O. B. and Deb Hoagland, Sister Kate and Uncle Adam Myers, Troy and Scott Allen, and our brood of cousins: Jenna, Alex, Zev, Ellie, and Quinn. Eternal gratitude goes to my wife, Eryn, who is as loving, patient, smart, creative, funny, generous, and encouraging a partner as any desert rat might dream of having. I often tell our daughters, Hannah and Caroline, that "it takes a family to make a book." It is for this reason that *Raising Wild* was dedicated to them. Indeed, the dedication of a book is the most sincere gesture of gratitude available to a writer. I have dedicated *Rants from the Hill* to my parents, Stu and Sharon Branch, who have directly or indirectly enabled everything I've accomplished in life. Without their support, the hill from which I rant would have remained a dream deferred, rather than one realized.

ABOUT THE AUTHOR

MICHAEL P. BRANCH is a professor of literature and environment at the University of Nevada, Reno, where he teaches creative nonfiction, American literature, environmental studies, and film studies. He has published seven books and more than two hundred essays, articles, and reviews, and his creative nonfiction includes pieces that have received honorable mention for the Pushcart Prize and been recognized as "notable essays" in *The Best American Essays* (three times), *The Best American Science and Nature Writing,* and *The Best American Nonrequired Reading* (a humor anthology). His work has appeared in many book-length essay collections, and in magazines including *Orion, Ecotone, Utne Reader, Slate, Places, Whole Terrain,* and *Red Rock Review.* His recent book, *Raising Wild: Dispatches from a Home in the Wilderness,* was released in 2016 by Shambhala's Roost Books imprint and is distributed by Penguin Random House.

Mike lives with his wife, Eryn, and daughters, Hannah Virginia and Caroline Emerson, in a passive-solar home of their own design at 6,000 feet on a hilltop in the remote high desert of northwestern Nevada, in the ecotone where the Great Basin Desert and Sierra Nevada Mountains meet. There he writes, plays blues harp, drinks sour mash, curses at baseball on the radio, cuts stove wood, and walks at least 1,200 miles each year in the surrounding, hills, canyons, ridges, arroyos, and playas.

For more on Mike Branch and his work, please visit his website at http://michaelbranchwriter.com.